RECORD BREAKERS
of the NFL

Thirteen action-packed accounts of the men who rewrote football's record book. Included are O.J. Simpson, Franco Harris, Johnny Unitas, Gale Sayers, and many other National Football League stars.

THE PUNT PASS AND KICK NFL LIBRARY

illustrated with photographs

RECORD BREAKERS
of the NFL

BY HOWARD LISS

RANDOM HOUSE • NEW YORK

Library of Congress Cataloging in Publication Data
Liss, Howard.   Record breakers of the NFL.   (Punt, pass & kick library)
SUMMARY: Describes thirteen performances by teams and individual players that set records in professional football.
1. Football—History—Juvenile literature. 2. Football—Biography—Juvenile literature. 3. National Football League—History—Juvenile literature. [1. Football—History. 2. National Football League—History. 3. Football—Biography] I. Title.
GV954.L57   796.33'264   [920]   75-8081
ISBN 0-394-83099-7   ISBN 0-394-93099-1 lib. bdg.

Published under license from National Football League Properties, Inc.
Manufactured in the United States of America   1 2 3 4 5 6 7 8 9 0

PHOTOGRAPH CREDITS: Vernon J. Biever, 48, 52; The Detroit Lions, Inc., 57; Malcolm W. Emmons, 2, 7, 16, 18, 25, 32, 35, 39, 51, 69, 98, 115, 136; Emmons and Brockway, 129; United Press International, endpapers, 4, 21, 29, 43, 62, 76, 81, 87, 91, 93, 101, 107, 112, 118, 120, 125, 143; Wide World Photos, 12–13, 68, 73, 82, 109, 133, 144.

Cover photo by Neil Leifer

For my brother-in-law, ABE MEDWIN—

    a great football fan and a great friend.

CONTENTS

INTRODUCTION

The Official National Football League record manual devotes hundreds of pages to the records set by individuals and teams. Every rookie dreams of seeing his name entered in that book some day.

Not every record breaker is a superstar, however. While some records represent sustained efforts by veteran pros, others are established by ordinary players on the basis of just one game—or even one play—when everything clicked perfectly. The longest pass ever completed in the NFL covered 99 yards. Four quarterbacks share that record: Karl Sweetan of the Detroit Lions, and Frank Filchock, George Izo, and Sonny

Jurgensen, all of the Washington Redskins. Of the four, only Jurgensen consistently proved his greatness; the others were average passers who simply enjoyed one great moment.

On the other hand, many of pro football's immortals never set any records. Every old-time fan will agree that Hall-of-Famer Mel Hein, who played with the New York Giants in the 1930s and '40s, was one of the greatest centers in NFL history; and Kenny Kavanaugh of the Chicago Bears was an all-time great receiver. Yet neither man is mentioned in the record books.

Then there are the players who made it into the book—and wish they hadn't. For example, the New York Giants led the league in defense eight different times, allowing the fewest points in a season. That is the NFL record. But in 1966, the New Yorkers allowed their rivals 501 points. That is a record, too—and one the Giants would be glad to see broken by some other hapless team.

And so it is with the players and teams in this book. There are genuine superstars like Johnny Unitas and George Blanda, who racked up one record after another during their long and outstanding careers. But there is also quarterback Bert Jones, who capped off a mediocre 1974 season with one record-breaking game. You'll read about one of the best team efforts in football (the Oakland Raider defense in 1967) and the absolute worst (the Chicago Cardinals of the early 1940s).

As you can see, a new record can be cause for celebration—or despair. But win or lose, it is the *Record Breakers of the NFL* who provide many of pro football's most exciting moments.

FRANCO'S
ITALIAN
ARMY

Back in the days when baseball's Brooklyn Dodgers were playing at Ebbets Field, a bunch of their fans got together to form a new kind of musical group. They'd show up at home games, wearing straw or derby hats and vests. Whenever their beloved Dodgers staged a rally, they would play off key and set up a terrible racket. They called themselves "The Brooklyn Sym-Phony."

A Baltimore basketball fan known simply as "Dancing Harry" attended all the Bullet games in the late 1960s. He'd prance up and down the sidelines, cheering his team on and giving the "evil eye" to rivals. When his favorite player, Earl Monroe, was traded to the New York Knicks in 1971, Harry brought his act all the way to Madison Square Garden.

But when it came to having unusual boosters, no one had it over Pittsburgh running back Franco Harris.

11

12

Every time Franco played, his special fans would be in the stands. They always sat together and were easily recognizable in their World War II helmet liners, painted with the green, white, and red colors of the Italian flag. They called themselves "Franco's Italian Army."

Franco's Italian Army was organized by a Pittsburgh baker named Tony Stagno and a few of his Italian friends. But you didn't have to be from Pittsburgh to join the group—singer Frank Sinatra was an honorary member. You didn't even have to be Italian—there were plenty of black men in Franco's Army. But that

wasn't surprising, since Franco Harris was a black Italian-American.

Franco's father, Cad Harris, was a black man from Bolton, Mississippi. As an army cook stationed in Europe during World War II, Mr. Harris met and married a woman from a small town near Pisa, Italy. After the war was over, Cad Harris decided to remain in the army. Franco, one of nine children, was born at Fort Dix, New Jersey, in 1950.

At Penn State, Franco played in the same backfield with another fine running back, Lydell Mitchell. The two running backs worked together to make State an

With flags and banners waving, Franco's Italian Army salutes its hero, Pittsburgh running back Franco Harris.

unbeatable powerhouse. But although Franco and Mitchell were good friends, their personalities were completely different.

"Mitchell does things almost by instinct, but Harris is the thoughtful type," said Penn coach Joe Paterno, comparing his two stars. "If I told Mitchell to run through a brick wall, he'd say, 'Okay, coach,' and he'd run through the brick wall. If I said the same thing to Harris, he'd count the bricks first—and then he'd run through the brick wall."

When it came to running through a wall of defenders, Franco was a hard man to beat. In three varsity years at Penn he gained 2,002 yards on 380 carries and scored 24 touchdowns. In one 1969 game (against Boston College) he ran for 136 yards and scored three touchdowns. Franco scored a pair of touchdowns in the Senior Bowl and was named to the College All-Star team.

Pittsburgh scouts had placed him in the "can't miss" category. Their reports on the 6-foot-2, 230-pound back indicated that he was one of the best blockers in college ball. Not surprisingly, the Steelers selected Franco in the first round of the 1972 draft.

Right from the start, Pittsburgh fans fell in love with Franco. His mixed ethnic background and his incredible skill and hustle made him a standout in any crowd. In his rookie year, Franco gained 1,055 yards rushing. (That made him the first Steeler rusher to pass the 1,000-yard mark since 1964, when John Henry Johnson had turned the trick for the second time in his career.) Franco's best rookie game was against Buffalo, when he rushed for 138 yards and also caught a touchdown pass. Several polls named him Rookie of the Year in the

American Football Conference, and Offensive Rookie of the Year in the whole National Football League.

Franco and the Steelers made it to the 1972 AFC playoffs, where they faced the Oakland Raiders. In that game Franco was the undisputed star. With just 22 seconds left on the clock, the Steelers were trailing by a single point. Pittsburgh quarterback Terry Bradshaw dropped back to pass to his primary receiver, running back Johnny Fuqua. But Fuqua was covered and Bradshaw began to scramble around. Realizing that Bradshaw was in trouble, Franco moved out of the backfield and got into position to receive a pass. Bradshaw threw, and the ball seemed to deflect off several pairs of reaching hands. Franco reached out and grabbed it, then streaked into the end zone to score the winning points.

After his spectacular rookie season, Harris got off to a disappointing start in 1973. He was injured in training camp, and that slowed him down for a while. Then he tried too hard to get back in shape and hurt himself again. As a result, he missed the first two games of the regular season and saw only limited action in the next three. By the sixth game Harris was back in the starting line-up and back in top form. Despite the fact that he'd missed a big part of the season, he again led his team in rushing, picking up 698 yards. The Steelers made the playoffs again but were quickly eliminated by the Oakland Raiders.

In 1974 everything seemed to click for Franco and the Steelers. For the second time in three years, the big running back gained over 1,000 yards rushing. The Pittsburgh defense was also fantastic. Quarterback Terry Bradshaw started off slowly, but before the

Franco Harris: football's only black Italian-American superstar.

season ended, he proved himself to be one of the best passers in the league. In the playoffs, the Steelers beat Buffalo. Then they defeated their old rivals, the Oakland Raiders, gaining the right to meet the Minnesota Vikings in the Super Bowl at New Orleans.

Minnesota's "Purple People Eaters" defense was every bit as tough as Pittsburgh's, and they proved it the first time the Steelers got the ball. On Pittsburgh's first play, running back Rocky Bleier gained 3 yards over tackle. Then Franco lost a yard. On third down, Bradshaw tried to pass and was thrown for a loss by the Vikings' Bob Lurtsema.

Franco and Bleier found the going just as rough the next time Pitt gained possession. In fact, in the entire first period, Franco's biggest gain was a 14-yard dash off right tackle. In his other six carries he gained only 10 yards.

The Minnesota defense wasn't the only thing slowing Franco down. Both teams were having trouble with the rain-soaked artificial turf, which was unusually slick. A receiver would race out, try to cut, and fall into a puddle. Ball carriers would attempt to turn the corner on end sweeps, and their feet would just slip out from under them. When a player was tackled, his body might hit the ground and slide for five yards. It looked pretty funny to the fans, but Franco wasn't laughing.

For most of the second period, Franco, Bleier, and Bradshaw were bottled up by the Minnesota defense. But the Viking offense was having trouble, too. Pittsburgh's front line kept knocking down the Minnesota ball carriers and deflecting quarterback Fran Tarkenton's passes. Neither team was able to score until the middle of the second quarter. Then, with the Vikings

Harris makes one of his many gains in Super Bowl IX.

deep in their own territory, the usually reliable Fran Tarkenton tried to pitch back to running back Dave Osborn. But the ball slipped out of Fran's grasp and rolled back to the Minnesota goal line. There was a mad scramble, and Tarkenton got there first. He covered the ball with his body just over the goal line. The safety gave the Steelers a 2–0 lead.

With less than a minute to go in the half, Franco got his second big chunk of yardage. He broke over the left side, got away from a linebacker, and raced 25 yards before being hauled down by safety man Paul Krause. Although Pittsburgh couldn't score before the half ended, Franco had picked up 61 yards in twelve carries.

Franco started off fast and furious in the second half. Within two minutes, he was crowding the 100-yard mark. Rookie linebacker Marv Kellum recovered a Viking fumble on the kickoff, so the Steelers started on the Minnesota 30. On their second play Franco tore through a hole in the left side of the Viking line and streaked 24 yards. Then he carried around right end, but he lost 3. On the next play he got the ball for the third time. He streaked around left end, and went 9 yards into the end zone. Now the Steelers led, 9–0.

For the Vikings, things went from bad to worse in the third period. Tarkenton had been scrambling around all afternoon trying to evade the rush of the Pittsburgh line. Now he ran to his right and attempted to get off a pass. Steeler defender L. C. Greenwood leaped up and batted the ball into the air. Tarkenton managed to catch the ball before it touched the ground, then passed again to John Gilliam for a long gain. But the play was called back.

The irate Vikings and their coach protested the call. The referee explained that the ball had been thrown forward and then it had been caught. Therefore it was a *completed* pass, Tarkenton-to-Tarkenton. That meant that the ball was already dead when Tarkenton threw to Gilliam.

Meanwhile, Franco was having better luck adding numbers to his gains. He crossed the 100-yard mark with a 9-yard carry, then kept banging away for more short gains: 4 yards here, another 4 there, then 6 yards, 1 yard, 3 yards. By the end of the third quarter he had picked up 118 yards in 22 carries.

The record for most yards gained in a Super Bowl game was held by Larry Csonka of the Miami Dolphins. In the 1974 game, also against the Minnesota Vikings, Csonka had rushed for 145 yards in 33 carries. Now Franco Harris was only 27 yards away from that mark, and he still had a whole period left. He seemed a cinch to break the record.

But the first time he got the ball in the fourth quarter, Franco tried to sweep left end and was met by half of the Viking defense. Not only was he held to no gain, but he fumbled the ball away. Pittsburgh got the ball right back, however, when the Vikings' Chuck Foreman fumbled and the Steelers' "Mean" Joe Greene recovered.

Still, the best Franco could do on the next series of plays was add 8 yards to his total. The Steelers failed to get a first down, and Bobby Walden came in to punt. Walden's kick was blocked, and Terry Brown recovered in the end zone for a Viking touchdown. Pittsburgh's lead shrunk to 9–6.

With less than 5 minutes remaining, Bradshaw

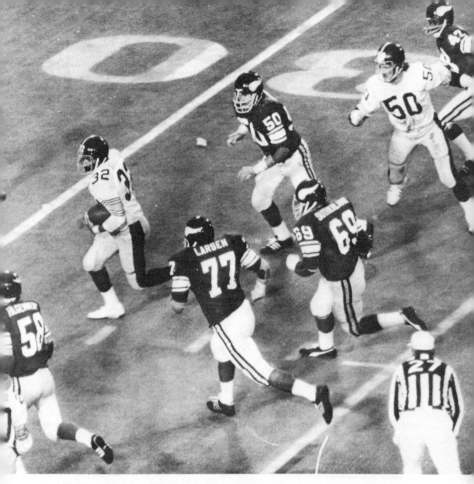

Franco (32) weaves his way through the Minnesota defense on the play that broke the Super Bowl rushing record.

engineered a twelve-play drive for a touchdown. On six of those plays Franco carried the ball, shoving his way forward, fighting for every inch of ground. The Minnesota defense had zeroed in on Franco, so Rocky Bleier was left free to break off right tackle for 17 yards. Then Bradshaw passed to Larry Brown for the touchdown.

By then Franco had gained 140 yards in 31 carries. With a little more than 2 minutes remaining and the

Steelers leading by 16–6, Franco had two jobs to do: first, help kill the clock to ensure the Steelers' victory; second, try to pick up at least 6 yards to beat Csonka's record.

Franco tried the left side for 2 yards, then the left side again for another yard. The 2-minute warning whistle blew, and the weary Harris knew he had to make his move. On the next play, he took the handoff, ran to his right, shook off a tackle, and bolted ahead for 15 big yards. The game ended with Pittsburgh still out front, 16–6. But the really big numbers were Franco's 158 yards gained in 34 carries—a new Super Bowl record.

As Harris trotted off the field the 81,000 fans in Tulane Stadium gave him a standing ovation. The next day Franco's achievement would make headlines in newspapers all over the country. But no one would appreciate his triumph more than a Pittsburgh baker named Tony Stagno and the other soldiers in Franco's Italian Army!

OLD
MAN
BLANDA

In April of 1974, Henry Aaron hit the 715th home run of his major league baseball career, breaking Babe Ruth's "unbreakable" record. After the cheering had died down, sportswriters noted an interesting fact about Aaron's achievement.

Several sluggers had hit 50 or more home runs during a season: Ralph Kiner did it twice, and so did Jimmy Foxx, Mickey Mantle, and Willie Mays. Yet none of them ever threatened Babe Ruth's record, while Henry Aaron (who never hit more than 47 in any season) was the man who broke it.

Aaron himself spelled out the reason for his success. He had simply played for more years than all the others. "If you hang around long enough," he said modestly, "something like this is bound to happen."

Undoubtedly, a football player named George Blanda would agree. By 1975, after more than a quarter of a century in the pros, the veteran passer held more NFL records than any other player in football history. And he accumulated many of his records by simply outlasting the competition, playing in more games, for more years, than anyone else.

During the early part of his career, however, Blanda seemed destined to set only one record: most minutes spent sitting on the bench. In 1949 he graduated from the University of Kentucky, where he had been the team's passer, punter, and place kicker. He wasn't drafted by the pros until the twelfth round, when the Chicago Bears decided to give him a chance. It was a slim chance at best, because the Bears already had three good quarterbacks—Sid Luckman, Johnny Lujack, and Bobby Layne.

Eventually, Layne was traded away, and Blanda became Chicago's third-string quarterback. Still, Blanda saw so little action during his first three pro years that he began to wonder why the Bears had bothered to draft him at all.

In his rookie year, quarterback Blanda tried only 21 passes and completed nine. In his second year he tried exactly one pass and didn't complete it. In his third year he didn't get off a single pass.

It was obvious that Blanda didn't have much of a future as a quarterback with Chicago. He had been a pretty fair college kicker, so it seemed he might have a better chance to do the punting and place kicking. But the Bears already had good punters—first George Gulyanics and then Curly Morrison. That left only place kicking. But even there Chicago had Johnny Lujack. He took care of the extra point attempts and the field goals from close range. So Blanda had to settle

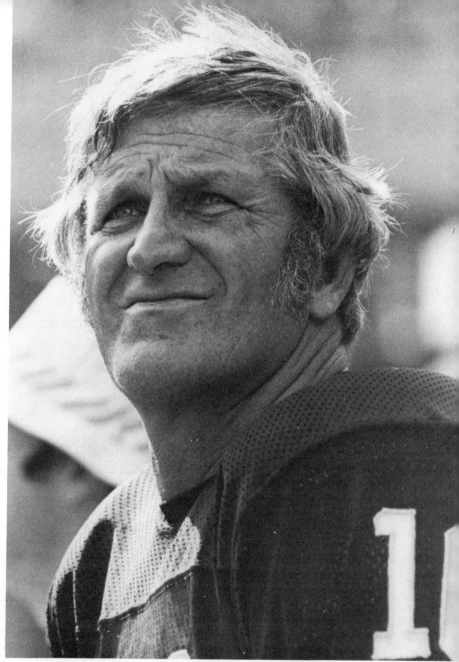

George Blanda: The Oakland Raiders' Grand Old Man.

for kicking off or trying the field goals from 35 or 45 yards out.

Desperate for more playing time, Blanda finally asked to be placed on the defensive team. So for a while he played lineback or cornerback. But his main contribution to the Bears was his point-after-touchdown kicking. From 1951 through 1958 he made 247 attempts, missing only three.

By 1953 Sid Luckman and Johnny Lujack had retired, and it looked as if Blanda might finally get his long-awaited chance to start at quarterback. The only players ahead of him were someone named Steve Romanik and a promising rookie named Tommy O'Connell, who had played on the Illinois Rose Bowl team. O'Connell started for the first two games, but he couldn't move the team. Then it was Blanda's turn to show what he could do as a starter.

That year Blanda led the NFL in passing attempts with 362. He completed 169, and 14 of those went for touchdowns. Although the Bears had a losing season, Blanda was sure he had the quarterback job locked up. He thought he had proved himself to be a major league passer. But owner-coach George Halas had other ideas. At the end of the season he promptly drafted two more quarterbacks: Zeke Bratkowski of Georgia and Ed Brown of the University of San Francisco.

Bratkowski was the starting quarterback in Chicago's first game of the 1954 season. It was a squeaker until the last 4 minutes, when a Bratkowski pass was intercepted and the Bears lost.

In the next game, against Los Angeles, Halas decided to go back to Blanda. The quarterback had an outstanding afternoon, completing 28 passes for 338 yards. Four of the passes resulted in touchdowns. And the following week, against San Francisco, Blanda threw three scoring strikes to receiver Harlan Hill. Despite Blanda's fine effort, however, the Bears fell behind, 27–24, with only 8 seconds to play. Then George Halas sent in quarterback Ed Brown to play the halfback position.

With two quarterbacks in the Chicago backfield, the Forty-Niners should have anticipated what came next —the old "flea flicker" play. But they didn't. Blanda took the snap from center and handed off to Brown, who ran wide, stopped, and tossed a perfect shot to Harlan Hill on the 10-yard line. Hill coasted in and the Bears won.

The next week, against Green Bay, the Bears were losing, 23–21, with 2 minutes left to play. Blanda threw the winning touchdown pass to Johnny Hoffman to put Chicago ahead, 28–23.

After four frustrating years, George's future was finally looking bright. But then in the very next game, against Cleveland, disaster struck. Two Cleveland defensemen caught the passer in a sandwich when his protection fell apart, and Blanda hobbled off the field with a shoulder separation.

For the next four years Blanda saw little service in the backfield. Mostly he was used as a place kicker. In 1956 he led the league in points-after-touchdown and field-goal tries, and the following year he again attempted more field goals than anyone else in the league. But he was getting older, and the kids were coming up from the colleges to challenge him even for the third-string quarterback job.

By 1959 it seemed that time had run out for George

Blanda. The Bears had three other passers, all younger: Bratkowski, Brown, and Rudy Bukich. That didn't leave much room for Blanda.

Halas gave Blanda three choices. He could try to make the team, but he would be third-stringer at best. And he would do no kicking, because Halas liked the looks of a rookie named John Aveni. Or, he might be traded, which meant moving his family out of Chicago. Or, he would be paid $6,000 a year just to keep in shape, in case the Bears needed his services.

Blanda agreed to wait for the call to action, but the call never came. He didn't play at all in 1959, a wasted year.

Now he was 32 years old and apparently all washed up in pro football. From 1955 through 1958 the Bears had not considered him good enough to be their starting passer. And in '59 he hadn't played at all, so even his kicking figured to be rusty. Who wanted a washed-up, third-string, out-of-practice football player? Nobody in the NFL, that much was sure.

Then in 1960 the American Football League was organized. In need of seasoned players to round out rosters made up primarily of inexperienced rookies, several of the newly formed teams remembered the veteran quarterback. The Houston Oilers got to Blanda first and made him an offer he gladly accepted.

Blanda spent the next seven years in Houston doing everything he had wanted to do with the Chicago Bears. As the Oilers' first-string passer and place kicker, he led the AFL in one department or another in almost every one of those years. Passes attempted, passes completed, touchdowns, points-after-touchdown, field-goal attempts—George did it all.

Playing for Houston in 1961, Blanda (16) gets off a pass despite the San Diego Chargers' aggressive defense.

Unfortunately, while Blanda was getting better and better, the Oilers were getting worse. After a winning start the first few years, Houston went into a slump. The once proud divisional champs became chronic tail-enders. In 1966 the Oilers finished the season with a dismal 3–11 record. By then Blanda's arm, which had thrown 2,784 passes in the last seven years, was aching, as a 39-year-old arm might well hurt. Suddenly he was no longer a hero to the fans. He was released by Houston, and once again his career seemed to be finished.

But the Oakland Raiders believed there was still some mileage left in the throwing arm and the kicking foot of George Blanda. So in 1967 he became the Raiders' second-line quarterback, and their first-line place kicker.

In Blanda's first year with Oakland, he led the league in conversions with 56 and hit on 20 out of 30 field-goal attempts. Furthermore, he completed 15 out of 38 passes, good for 285 yards and three touchdowns. Oakland won the American Football League championship.

Like Old Man River, Old Man Blanda kept rolling along. He was 41 years old in 1968, his second year with the Raiders, but he hit with 54 extra points and 21 out of 34 field goals. As a back-up passer, he was 30-for-49, gaining 522 yards with six touchdowns. In 1969 he made 45 conversions and added another 20 field goals to his total. As a quarterback, he tried only 13 passes but connected with six, for 73 yards and two TDs.

Then in 1970 a funny thing happened. The American Football League merged with the National Football League. All previous records of both leagues counted in the new record book. And lo and behold! George Blanda's name led all the rest!

Once Lou "The Toe" Groza of the Cleveland Browns had held all the place-kicking records, the record for most points. But suddenly the records belonged to George Blanda. He had played more years than anybody else, more games than anybody else. And he wasn't done yet.

Blanda was 43 years old when the 1970 season got under way. By the time the year was over, football fans everywhere had a new hero, a gray-haired gentleman who was making the game look like child's play. Time after time that season, the Raiders relied on Blanda's experience in the clutch. And every time, he came through when they needed him most.

In the sixth game of the season, Oakland was tied with Pittsburgh at 7–all when first-string passer Daryle Lamonica was injured. Blanda replaced him. On his first play, he calmly dropped back and zinged the ball to tight end Ray Chester for a 29-yard touchdown. Before the afternoon ended Blanda had racked up a scoring pass to Warren Wells, another touchdown pass to Chester, and a field goal. Thanks to Blanda, Oakland romped to a 31–14 victory.

Next came tough Kansas City. With Lamonica back at the helm, the Raiders were behind, 17–14. The ball was on the KC 41-yard line with just seconds to go. Blanda came out to try the long field goal with the wind against him. He took the hop-step and put his toe into the ball with all he had. It flipped up and out, sailed half the length of the field, and barely cleared the crossbar. The game ended in a tie.

In the early 1970s, Blanda did double duty for the Raiders, passing and kicking. Here he boots the ball over the crossbar for an extra point.

The Cleveland Browns followed, and as the last period began, they led Oakland, 17–13. Once again Lamonica was hurt and Blanda came in. But now the Raiders needed more than a field goal to save the game. It looked as if the old-timer's luck had finally run out. Blanda threw an interception, and the Browns cashed it in for a field goal, making the score 20–13.

But Blanda was not about to give up. He came right back, throwing completions to Warren Wells, Charlie Smith, and Hewritt Dixon, moving the ball closer and closer to the Cleveland goal. Even when he was sacked behind the line for a loss of 10 yards, Blanda didn't lose his cool. He stayed in the air, connecting with Fred Biletnikoff and finally with Warren Wells for the tying TD to make the score 20–20.

With a minute left in the game, Cleveland tried to get within field-goal range with quick moves downfield. But Bill Nelsen was intercepted and Oakland took over. Then Blanda tried to move the Raiders, but his passes were incomplete. With 3 seconds left the Raiders had the ball on Cleveland's 45.

Now Oakland's only hope for a win was a field goal from 52 yards out! Blanda bashed the ball with his toe and it sailed up and out and over the crossbar. Once again the old pro had pulled a game out of the fire.

Then it was Denver's turn to see what the veteran could do. The Broncos were leading, 19–17, when Blanda went into the game with 4 minutes to play. The enemy goal was 80 long yards away.

Blanda's first play lost 2 yards. His next play was an incomplete pass. Then with third and 12 on his own 18, he nailed receiver Rod Sherman with a 27-yarder for the first down. A pass to Warren Wells, good for 35 more yards, put the ball on the Denver 20.

A less experienced quarterback might have tried to run out the clock with a couple of ground plays, then booted the easy field goal for the go-ahead point. But that could have left Denver with enough time to take the kickoff, move ahead to field goal range, and win the game in the final seconds.

Blanda elected to gamble. He threw an incompletion. On the next play Oakland was offside, but the Broncos declined the penalty. They knew the yardage would make little difference in Blanda's kick. Denver preferred to take the down, thus giving Oakland less time to control the ball. They still figured to hang on, give Blanda the field goal, then try to get their own field goal in the final seconds of the game.

That was their mistake. On the next play Blanda saw Biletnikoff in the open and put the ball into his hands on the goal line. Touchdown! Now it was 24–19, and a field goal couldn't help Denver any longer. They had to go all the way, and they didn't make it.

The Raiders' next contest was against San Diego. This time, with 16 seconds left, Blanda booted the field goal that gave Oakland a 20–17 victory.

Weeks later, against the Jets, Blanda hit with a touchdown pass and kicked a pair of extra points to give his team a 14–13 triumph.

That year Oakland finished with an 8–4–2 record, the best in their division. And that year 43-year-old George Blanda—the man released by two teams in two different leagues—won the NFL's MVP Award and was voted Man of the Year by *Sport* magazine.

And still he didn't quit. He came back to the Raiders in 1971, 1972, 1973, and 1974. And game after game, the numbers kept piling up.

By the end of the 1974 season a look through the record book revealed that George Blanda had set or tied the mark in no fewer than 16 different categories:

Most seasons as an active player: 25
Most games, lifetime: 326
Most consecutive games, lifetime: 210
 (Tied with Jim Otto)

The 47-year-old Blanda takes it easy for a change during a 1974 practice session.

Most points, lifetime: 1,919
Most seasons leading league in points-after-touchdown: 7
Most points-after-touchdown attempted, lifetime: 911
Most points-after-touchdown scored, lifetime: 899
Most points-after-touchdown attempted, one season: 65
Most points-after-touchdown scored, one season: 64
Most field goals attempted, lifetime: 627
Most field goals scored, lifetime: 322
Most passes attempted, one game: 68
Most passes completed, one game: 37
Most touchdown passes in one season: 36
    (Tied with Y.A. Tittle)
Most passes intercepted, lifetime: 276
Most passes intercepted, one season: 42

George Blanda was proud of his records, even the ones showing how often his passes were intercepted. For they proved that he was always challenging the defenses, willing to throw even when they knew he would and were waiting in ambush.

When an athlete gets older, his legs are supposed to give out. But Blanda's legs got stronger, and his eye sharper, as he booted the ball over the uprights from all distances, all angles. Looking forward to the 1975 season, George Blanda explained his success to an interviewer. "I'm not too old," he said. "The other players are too young."

THE DAY
THE FOOTBALLS
FLEW

When the Minnesota Vikings collided with the Baltimore Colts at Met Stadium in Bloomington, Minnesota, on September 29, 1969, even the most inexperienced fans knew roughly what kind of game to expect. All they had to do was study the line-ups.

Both clubs had great front fours. For the Vikings it was the notorious "Purple People Eaters": Carl Eller, Gary Larsen, Jim Marshall, and Alan Page, as fearsome a group as any in the game. The Colts also had a fine line consisting of Roy Hilton and big Bubba Smith at ends, and Billy Ray Smith and Fred Miller at tackles. Faced with such powerful defenses, neither side figured to do much running.

When it came to a passing game, Baltimore seemed to have the edge. Their number-one quarterback was Johnny Unitas, the greatest passer in NFL history.

Backing him up was Earl Morrall, once considered merely a journeyman thrower. But the previous season, when Unitas was injured, the Colts had been forced to rely on Morrall. The second-stringer had risen to the occasion and led his team all the way to the Super Bowl. So now Baltimore's aerial attack was in very good hands.

The Vikings also had a pretty good passer in Gary Cuozzo. A former Colt, he had spent several frustrating years playing second fiddle behind Unitas. At the time, he was considered the best second-stringer in the league. When the Vikings finally got him in 1968, they considered themselves lucky.

The Vikings' back-up passer, Joe Kapp, was not considered much of a threat, however. According to the experts, he couldn't do anything right. He tended to throw off the wrong foot, and he was considered too much of a scrambler. In fact, he liked to run into people. Most quarterbacks, when forced out of the pocket, would run for their lives, heading for the sidelines where they couldn't get tackled. Seeing a big linebacker barreling toward them, they would fall gracefully to the ground and lie there, praying. But not Joe Kapp.

When Kapp had to scramble, he would do his best to impersonate a fullback and run straight at a tackler. Then, more often than not, Kapp would bounce up, grinning, before the puzzled tackler could figure out what hit him.

Before the game started, several Baltimore players told reporters that they hoped Viking coach Bud Grant would start Joe Kapp at quarterback. Many of the

Joe Kapp, Minnesota's back-up passer, begins a long day of work against the Baltimore Colts.

Colts had been teammates of Cuozzo and they respected his arm. Kapp's arm, however, didn't seem to impress them at all. Surprisingly, the Colts got their wish—one they would heartily regret before the day was over.

On the first play from scrimmage, Joe Kapp came out throwing. As he dropped back, the whole Baltimore line converged on him. But Kapp scrambled around, saw Dave Osborn free, and hit him with the ball. The play was good for 31 yards. Kapp's next move was an 18-yard strike to wide receiver John Henderson. A draw by fullback Bill Brown gained a few more yards, and then Kapp fired to Osborn again for the touchdown. The series of four plays had taken exactly 2 minutes, 6 seconds. And three of the plays were completed passes.

The Colts opened their attack more cautiously. Preston Pearson and Tom Matte earned a first down running. Unitas' first pass was ruled complete when Minnesota safety Karl Kassulke interfered with John Mackey. But then the Colt quarterback's luck turned sour. Receiver Jimmy Orr dropped a pass, and the Viking front four forced a hurried incompletion. The Colts had to kick the ball away.

It took Joe Kapp only one play to add another touchdown to the Vikings' score. With the ball on his own 17, he let fly a long one. Gene Washington grabbed the pass on the Colt 45 and didn't stop running until he reached the end zone. After the conversion, Minnesota led, 14–0.

Unitas tried to get the Colts on the scoreboard with a series of passes. He completed one but missed with two others, and Baltimore had to punt. Kapp, on the other hand, completed two more (that made five straight completions for him). The Viking quarterback's string was finally broken when Bill Brown dropped the ball.

For the rest of the quarter both teams' air game collapsed. Unitas tried five more passes. Three were incomplete, one gained 3 yards, and another was intercepted.

Kapp's passing was even worse. He tried seven more but completed just one of them. Twice he was dropped for a loss as the Colt defense closed in on him. And one of his throws was intercepted by Colt linebacker Dennis Gaubatz.

When the second quarter began, both teams tried a ground attack, with no more success. Then Earl Morrall came in to replace Unitas and took to the air, hitting on just two of five passes. Kapp responded with four passing attempts and also completed two. Neither team was able to score.

Finally, with almost half of the second period gone, Baltimore got a break. Viking back Osborn fumbled, and Rick Volk recovered on the Colt 47. Now it was Morrall's turn to blitz through the air. A pass to running back Jerry Hill was good for 11 yards. Then Morrall spotted Tom Matte sneaking out of the backfield and hit him for 43 yards and the touchdown. Now the score was 14–7, Vikings.

Morrall's success seemed to be contagious. Immediately after the kickoff, Joe Kapp regained his own touch. The Vikings started from their own 22. Joe used eleven plays to lead them to the end zone, and eight of those were passes. Kapp used five different receivers: Bill Brown, John Beasley, Gene Washington, Jim Lindsey, and finally Bob Grim, who grabbed the touchdown heave.

Now the Colts were behind by two touchdowns (21–7), and Morrall knew they'd really be out of the ballgame if he didn't act fast. The Colts' running attack was going nowhere, so once more their quarterback went to the air. Morrall tried three passes. The first was good, the second was no good, and the third was worst of all—it was intercepted.

When the ball went over to Minnesota, Joe Kapp also tried three passes. The first was batted down, and the other two gained a total of only 4 yards. Fortunately, the Vikings were in field goal range, and Fred Cox booted one from 40 yards out to put the Vikings ahead 24–7.

Morrall was getting desperate, and his play showed it. He got off just one pass, which was picked off, and the weary Baltimore defense went back onto the field. They were in no condition to stop Kapp. He threw four times, and the Vikings had another touchdown.

It was a long, bitter day for Baltimore. Unitas went back into the line-up, but he was no more successful than Morrall had been. Johnny U tried to pass three times but couldn't hit anybody. The Colts punted, giving Kapp the ball again.

With his team ahead 31–7, a more conservative quarterback might have played it safe and tried to use up the remaining time with short but steady ground gains. But Joe Kapp was having too much fun with his passing game to switch tactics now. It seemed as if he could do no wrong.

Once, he dropped back, was chased out of the pocket, and scrambled for a gain of 10 yards. Just before he was tackled, Kapp lateraled to Dave Osborn, who picked up another 3. On another play, Joe seemed to be trapped behind the Colt line. But he dodged away from a sure tackle and unleashed a 45-yarder to Gene Washington for another touchdown.

Baltimore's Johnny Unitas (19) gets off a pass just before he's reached by the Viking defense.

Now Baltimore was behind 38–7, and Unitas' only hope was to hang in there and keep throwing. Sooner or later he was bound to get it all together. And that's just what he did on the series that followed. In seven plays (five were completed passes), he took the Colts all the way to the end zone.

And still Joe Kapp kept passing. It took eleven plays to score another TD; five were passes. Now it was 45–14, Vikings.

With the game locked up, Kapp took a rest and Gary Cuozzo came in. He lofted a few throws of his own but had to leave the field when he suffered a broken nose on one pass rush. Back came Kapp, who was still warmed up. The pass-happy quarterback picked up right where he'd left off—with two more throws, good for still another touchdown.

Later Bob Lee, Minnesota's third-string passer, took over for Kapp, while Morrall subbed for Unitas. Both quarterbacks took turns throwing the ball, but neither team was able to score again. At last, the tossing contest ended with the Vikings on top, 52–14. The autumn birds of Minnesota, which had been chased out of the sky by flying footballs, soared above the field once more. And the Vikings went home with their most decisive victory in a long time.

Only the game's statisticians remained where they were. Their work was just beginning. Not counting kickoffs, punts, runbacks, or penalties, Baltimore had possession for 58 plays. Only 16 of those had been ground plays; an incredible 42 had been passes. In 22 attempts, Unitas had connected on eight, while Morrall had completed twelve of 20. Altogether, the Baltimore offense had gained 251 yards: 56 on the ground, and 195 in the air.

Minnesota had kept the ball for 83 plays, and 56 of those were passes. Kapp had gone 28-for-43, Cuozzo 4-for-7, and Bob Lee 4-for-6. The three quarterbacks had gained a total of 538 yards in the air.

Altogether, Baltimore and Minnesota had thrown a total of 98 passes, shattering the passing record for two teams in a single game. But that wasn't all. Joe Kapp personally tied a record. His seven touchdown throws equaled the mark held by Adrian Burke, Y.A. Tittle, and Sid Luckman. No one could deny that Joe Kapp had gotten off on the right foot that day.

SUPER-ROOKIE
SAYERS

The Chicago Bears' scouting report on Gale Sayers read, "Halfback, great speed, great prospect, should be graded in the 'one' category." And no wonder. Sayers' record at the University of Kansas had been spectacular. In his three varsity years, he had rushed for 2,675 yards, or 6.5 yards per carry. He had returned punts 28 times for 342 yards and carried 22 kickoffs back for 513 yards. He was also an excellent receiver, snaring 35 passes for another 408 yards. Those kinds of statistics made Sayers an obvious All-America choice during his last two college years—and an obvious pro prospect.

Sayers came to the Bears in 1965, the team's number one draft choice. Almost immediately, he began living up to his rave notices. A minor injury kept the rookie out of the line-up for most of the Bears' first two pre-season games. But in the third exhibition game, against the Los Angeles Rams, Sayers finally got a chance to show what he could do. He ran back a kickoff 93 yards, traveled 77 yards with a punt, and caught a 25-yard pass. To top it all off, he tossed an option pass for a touchdown.

When the regular season opened, however, Sayers was not in the starting backfield. Ranked ahead of him were veteran Jon Arnett, as well as Andy Livingston and Ron Bull. Against San Francisco, Sayers was used sparingly. He got the ball only five times and picked up just 30 yards.

Sayers didn't do much in Chicago's second game either. Against the Rams, he returned a couple of kickoffs, one of them for 42 yards. But he did score a touchdown on an 18-yard run.

Since the Bears had lost both games, coach George Halas decided it was time to let his prize rookie see a little more action. So when Chicago faced the mighty Green Bay Packers in game three, Sayers was in the starting line-up. In the third period he went over from 6 yards out to score the first Chicago touchdown. Then, late in the fourth quarter, he caught two passes. One was good for 16 yards, the other for 65 yards and the Bears' second TD. Chicago lost the game, 24–14, but Sayers had shown that he was truly a winner.

When the Rams came visiting for the fourth regular season game, they ran into the same Gale Sayers who had given them a hard time in the exhibition game. Late in the third quarter, Chicago was clinging to a scant 10–6 lead. The Bears found themselves in a second-and-20 situation with the ball on their own 20-yard line. Quarterback Rudy Bukich dropped back and floated a screen pass to Sayers, who took off

Early in the 1965 season, Chicago rookie Gale Sayers (40) shows what he can do against the Green Bay Packers.

toward the goal. He broke Chuck Lamson's tackle, survived a shot from 285-pound Roosevelt Grier, and ran 80 yards into the end zone.

In the fourth quarter, Sayers worked the option pass to receiver Dick Gordon for 29 yards and another touchdown to help give the Bears a 31–6 victory, their first of the season.

In game five, Minnesota kept Sayers bottled up for most of the first three periods, and the Vikings took an early lead. But seconds before the third quarter ended,

Sayers finally cut loose. With the ball on Minnesota's 16, he took a Bukich pass on the 5, squirmed free of a tackle, and went in for the touchdown. Then, on Chicago's first series of plays in the fourth period, he caught a 25-yard pass for another score.

But the Vikings weren't about to play dead. The lead seesawed throughout the final quarter. With 2½ minutes left, Minnesota's Bill Brown plunged 4 yards for a touchdown to give the Vikings a 37–31 edge.

Fred Cox kicked off to Chicago and booted a long one out to Sayers on the 4-yard line. The speedy rookie cut to the sidelines, put on a couple of beautiful fakes, broke a tackle, and dashed 96 yards to pay dirt. Sayers closed out the day with a run over right guard for 10 yards and another touchdown, his fourth of the afternoon, to wrap up the game for Chicago.

Sayers scored a touchdown in each of the next two games, against Detroit and Green Bay. It had been a remarkable half-season for the rookie running back. After being shut out in the opener, he had scored ten touchdowns in the next six games.

In game eight, however, Sayers and the Bears ran into a determined Baltimore team. Maybe Gale Sayers was due for a let-down game. Or maybe the Colts keyed in on Sayers to protect the record of teammate Lenny Moore, who had scored a record-breaking 20 touchdowns the previous season. Whatever the reason, Sayers was hounded everywhere he tried to run, and had no chance to score. In fact, Gale gained only 17 yards rushing in eleven carries. He caught a few passes, one good for 31 yards, and he ran back some kickoffs. But it was a bad day all around, as Sayers and the Bears bowed to Baltimore, 26–21.

In the game against St. Louis the following week, Sayers had some trouble regaining his momentum—at least for the first few minutes. With the ball on the Chicago 41, he fumbled, and the Cards recovered on the 37. Then Cardinal quarterback Charley Johnson flipped a pass to receiver Sonny Randle, who went all the way.

Sayers' error was forgotten on the very next play, however. St. Louis' Jim Bakken kicked off, and Sayers took the ball just short of the goal line. He tore up the middle, cut to the sidelines, broke free, and twisted his way down the field. He went all the way to the St. Louis 13 before he was nailed from behind. Two plays later the Bears had tied the score.

By the time the fourth quarter got underway, Chicago was leading, 17–13. Then Gale and the Bears really got down to business. On one drive, Chicago used 14 plays—and Sayers was involved in half of them. With the ball on the 7-yard line, he went over left tackle for the touchdown.

Sayers continued his scoring spree when Chicago faced the Lions in the following game. The score was tied at 10–10 when he swept right end, eluded three tackles, and went over the big chalk line. The Bears moved ahead, 17–10. That was all the scoring for the day. Sayers' touchdown had won the ballgame.

Sayers was double trouble for the New York Jets in game eleven. First he caught a pitchout for a 10-yard touchdown run around left end. Later he ran a straight end sweep for another 15 yards and his second TD.

Chicago's next game was a rematch against the Baltimore Colts. But this time, Sayers was not about to be stopped. In the first period, with the ball on

A mud-spattered Sayers manages to hold on to the slippery ball during a 1965 game.

Sayers watches the action from the bench with coach George Halas.

Chicago's 39, he took the pitchout from Bukich. Sayers swung outside right end, got away from defensive back Bob Boyd, and sailed 61 yards down the sidelines for the score.

By now, Gale Sayers was the idol of Chicago. In twelve games he had scored 15 touchdowns—and put the Bears on the winning side of the ledger. But in the next game, against the Forty-Niners, Sayers showed that he was just beginning to move.

The rookie runner got off to a fast start in the first period. Chicago quarterback Bukich tried two passes, both incomplete, so the Bears had a third-and-10 situation on their own 20. Then Bukich dropped back and flipped a soft screen pass to Sayers out in the flat. The halfback followed his blockers, then sped out front to post an 80-yard touchdown.

In the second period Sayers scored twice more, once on a 21-yard end sweep and again on a 7-yard run. In the third quarter he took a pitchout and broke through for 50 yards and his fourth touchdown of the day. Later in that same period, Sayers went over the goal for number five. But this time it was a pure power play, as he plunged through the middle from a yard out.

Midway through the fourth quarter Sayers struck again. He fielded a punt on his own 15-yard line, veered to the sidelines, and sprinted 85 yards for TD number six. With that touchdown, Gale Sayers had already tied the record for most scores in a single game. He had also broken Lenny Moore's record by scoring his 21st touchdown of the season.

With Chicago leading, 54–20, Coach Halas motioned his rookie to the bench. But when another Chicago drive took the ball to the San Francisco 2-yard line, first-and-goal for the Bears, 43,000 Bear fans screamed for Halas to put Sayers back into the game so that he could score his seventh touchdown and break the record.

Coach George Halas did not budge. He watched as Bukich threw an incompletion, and then as Jon Arnett cracked over for the score to make the score 61–20.

Just before time ran out, the fans thought Sayers might break the record anyway. He came in for a punt return, caught the ball on his own 19, and ran it back 30 yards before being stopped by the whole San Francisco team. The game ended before Sayers or the Bears could score again.

Later, in the dressing room, Halas was asked why he had not permitted Sayers to go in for a shot at the record-breaking seventh touchdown.

"Nobody was hungrier than I was to have Sayers score number seven," Halas replied. "But we had it clinched already. What if he'd been hurt? I'd never forgive myself."

Sayers didn't bemoan his missed opportunity. "It wouldn't have done me any good," he explained. "The Forty-Niners knew the game was lost. If I'd come back, they would have known why I was on the field, and they'd have been ready for me."

Sayers finished out the season with still another TD, this one against the Vikings on a 2-yard slant over right tackle. That gave him an incredible total of 22 touchdowns for the season, two more than any player in NFL history. But if anyone was surprised at the super-rookie's showing, it wasn't the Chicago scouts. They'd known from the very start that Gale Sayers was Number One!

PRO
FOOTBALL'S
WORST TEAMS

In 1960 the National Football League was expanded to include the new Dallas Cowboys franchise. That year the Cowboys didn't win a game, although they did manage to eke out one tie. Disappointed fans called Dallas the worst team in NFL history. But according to the record book, they weren't even close. When it came to losing, the Detroit Lions and Chicago Cardinals of the 1940s were best of all.

The Detroit Lions of the late 1930s and early '40s were hardly world-beaters, but they certainly weren't the worst team in the league. Coached by Bill Edwards, they generally won about as many games as they lost. The Lions had some decent players in running backs Ned Mathews and Mickey Sanzotta, plus one of the greatest of all centers, Alexander Wojciechowicz. Going into the 1942 season, they figured to have another fair season.

Detroit opened against the Chicago Cardinals and picked up their first defeat of the season, a 13–0 shutout. The Lions couldn't stop rookie passer Bud Schwenk, who connected on two touchdown passes, one to rookie Steve Lach, the other to end Bill Daddio. Detroit's offense went nowhere.

Game two, against the Cleveland Rams, was no better for the Lions. Once, they managed to get the ball to the Cleveland 3-yard line. But four plays later they had lost 1 yard and Cleveland took over on downs. The Lions chalked up their second loss, a 14–0 shutout.

The Lions lost their third game—against the Brooklyn Dodgers—but it wasn't easy. The Dodgers tried desperately to hand the game over on a silver platter, fumbling the ball six times. But Detroit couldn't capitalize on Brooklyn's mistakes. One fumble was recovered by Detroit on the Brooklyn 12. Ned Mathews and Mickey Sanzotta fired passes to receivers who were in the clear. But each time, the ball hit the intended receiver in the chest and fell to the ground. The Lions finally got on the scoreboard, but Brooklyn won anyway, by a score of 28–7.

The Lions started their fourth game with a new coach, John "Bull" Karcis, and for a few minutes it looked as if their jinx might be broken. Against mighty Green Bay, Detroit took a surprising 7–3 first quarter lead. But then the Packers really began to press. Green Bay's halfback Emil Banjovic ripped off a 45-yard run, and a short time later fullback Elmer Hackney scored from 9 yards out. After that the Pack's Hall-of-Fame combination of quarterback Cecil Isbell and receiver

The Detroit Lions had little to smile about when this team photograph was taken during the 1942 season.

Don Hutson took the game out of reach. Final score: 38–7, Green Bay.

In a return match against the Chicago Cardinals, Detroit was completely helpless. The final score was 7–0, and the Lions were just lucky it wasn't a lot worse. The Cards scored their only points on a 59-yard dash by fullback Bob Morrow. But four other times they penetrated the Lion defense and got inside the Detroit 20. Fortunately for Detroit, Cardinal place kicker Bill

Daddio never could connect for a field goal. The Lions, on the other hand, never even threatened to score. Once, halfback Harry Hopp ran 44 yards to the Chicago 36, but that was the farthest any Lion got all day.

The Lions' sixth game of the season was a rematch against the Packers, and once more Detroit took an early 7–0 lead, moving 80 yards in 17 plays for a touchdown. On the following kickoff, Green Bay's Andy Uram fielded the ball on his own 1-yard line and raced 99 yards into the Detroit end zone to tie the game. The Lions tried hard to regain the lead, but nothing seemed to work. As far as statistics went, Detroit had the best of it. They had sixteen first downs to the Packers' nine, 152 yards on the ground to 48, and 128 yards in the air to 118. But the most important figures—points scored—were gained by the Packers, who won 28–7.

More Detroit losses followed: to the Bears by 16–0, to Pittsburgh by 35–7, to Cleveland by 27–7. Then, in another game against the Bears, the Lions went from bad to worse. Detroit fumbled five times; and each time, the ball was recovered by the Bears.

The action became so helter-skelter that even the referees had trouble following the game. At one point, they actually gave Chicago a fifth down! League Commissioner Elmer Layden happened to be in the stands watching the game, but even he could do nothing about the situation, because—right or wrong —the officials are always *right*. Anyway, Chicago hardly needed the advantage as they slaughtered the Lions, 42–0.

For Detroit, the season ended as it had begun—with

a defeat. After their 15–13 loss to the Washington
Redskins, the Lions left the field with a season's record
of 0–11–0. Of course, it wasn't the first time a National
Football League team had gone winless during a
season. The Cincinnati Gunners-Reds had done that in
1934, but they only played eight games.

In the eleven games of '42, Detroit had been
outscored 263 to 38. Altogether the Lions had managed only five touchdowns and one field goal, never
more than one score per game. In five of the games
they hadn't even gotten on the scoreboard. It was hard
to imagine any team doing worse than that—but it
wasn't long before one did.

In 1942, the same year the Lions failed so miserably,
the Chicago Cardinals got off to a fast start with a pair
of shutouts over Cleveland and Detroit. Then they lost
to a couple of fine teams, the Green Bay Packers and
the Chicago Bears. But the Cardinals bounced back in
their fifth game with a 7–0 win over the hapless Lions.
Chicago didn't know it then, but it would be a long
time before they came up with their next victory.

The Cardinals' next game was against the Cleveland
Rams, and it was a thriller right down to the final gun.
Trailing by 7–3 late in the fourth quarter, Chicago
mounted a powerful drive. Rookie quarterback Bud
Schwenk passed to Marshall Goldberg, who took the
ball to the Cleveland 22. A pair of shots into the line
plus another pass, this time to Steve Lach, advanced
Chicago to the Cleveland 9. Lach then crashed to the
2, but the Lions were stopped there. They tried three
more cracks into the line but failed to get the ball into
the end zone.

Cleveland was unable to score either, and a booming

punt gave the ball back to the Cards on their own 43 with 3 minutes to play. Again Schwenk took his team back into Cleveland territory. Twelve of the next 13 plays were passes and nine of them clicked. But once more, the Cardinals were stopped 2 yards short of the goal. The game ended with Chicago still on the losing end of a 7–3 score.

Nursing their bruises, the Cardinals went up against the Green Bay Packers and were picked apart, 55–24. But it really wasn't a disgrace. Green Bay's great Cecil Isbell was in top form that day. He tossed five touchdown passes, two to his magnificent running back, Andy Uram, and three more to his favorite receiver, the great Don Hutson.

Unfortunately, the Cardinals ran into another all-time passer the following week. This time it was Sammy Baugh of the Washington Redskins. He tossed three touchdown passes to help the 'Skins defeat Chicago, 28–0.

The Cards' final three games, against the Steelers, the Giants, and the Bears, were all losses. That gave them six defeats in a row, and a season's record of 3–8–0.

"Wait until next year," their loyal fans said, little knowing what lay ahead.

When the 1943 football season opened, the United States was heavily involved in World War II. So many players had joined the armed forces that the NFL had to be reorganized. Now there were eight teams instead of ten, and one of those was a combination of the old Pittsburgh Steelers and Philadelphia Eagles, renamed the Steagles. Just about every one of the remaining teams had lost some of its best talent to the war effort, so the competition didn't figure to be as stiff as it had been the year before.

The Chicago Cardinals opened the season against the Detroit Lions. Both teams had finished the previous season with losing streaks. And both teams had new coaches: Phil Handler had taken over for Jimmy Conzelman at the helm of the Cardinals, while Gus Dorais, a former Notre Dame star, had replaced John Karcis in Detroit.

It wasn't much of a contest. Detroit exploded for five touchdowns, which was exactly the number they had scored during the *entire* previous year. After eleven losses in '42, the Lions finally came out on top, beating Chicago 35–17. But Detroit's gain was Chicago's loss—their seventh in a row, to be precise.

The Cardinals' next game, against Green Bay, was even more discouraging. On one series of downs the Cards lost 11 yards in three plays. To top it off, their punt was blocked and recovered by the Packers for a loss of another 26 yards. Thus, the Cardinals actually went *backwards* 37 yards from the original line of scrimmage. After that, it took the Packers only six plays to score a touchdown.

Ron Cahill, Chicago's rookie passer, tried to get something going for his team, with little success. He attempted 20 passes and completed just eleven. Unfortunately, another five were intercepted, and the game ended with Green Bay ahead, 28–7.

As the season progressed, Chicago's losses mounted. The Cards fell before the Lions, the Redskins, the Steagles, and the Dodgers. Then came more defeats at the hands of Green Bay and the New York Giants.

The last game of the year pitted the Cardinals

against their hometown rivals, the Chicago Bears. The winless Cards were determined not to duplicate Detroit's horrible 1942 season, and for a time it looked as if they might finally snap their string of losses.

The Cards took a 7–0 lead on a short plunge by running back Johnny Grigas, but the Bears promptly tied the game with a touchdown and conversion of their own. Then Conway Baker kicked a field goal to give the Cards a 10–7 edge, but the Bears took back the lead with another TD. In the third period the Cards really got moving, scoring twice to lead, 24–14. But the Bears triumphed in the end when veteran Bronco Nagurski scored on a 1-yard plunge, and

Card-Pitt defender Walt Kichefski (white helmet) seems to be on his own against the Giants as his team chalks up another loss in 1944.

quarterback Sid Luckman threw two more touchdown passes. Final score: Bears, 35–Cardinals, 24.

Counting the six losses in a row that ended their 1942 season, and their ten straight defeats in '43, the Chicago Cardinals now held the pro football record of 16 consecutive losses. But the worst was still to come.

The 1944 season saw another team merger. This time it was Pittsburgh and Chicago. The Cards changed their name to Card-Pitt, and Cardinal fans hoped their team's luck would change, too. And it almost did in their opener as they lost a squeaker to the Cleveland Rams, 30–28.

Somewhat heartened, Card-Pitt took on the New York Giants in an exhibition game. After falling behind, 16–3, they suddenly caught fire and struck for two fast touchdowns that gave them a 17–16 win. Technically, of course, the game didn't count, and it wouldn't show up in the standings. But after 17 straight losses, even an unofficial victory was a hopeful sign. But all hopes were dashed when it mattered for the record. In their next two regular games, they bowed to Green Bay, 34–7, and were shut out by the Giants, 23–0. Defeat followed defeat as the team went through another year of bitterness. Again they lost every game. By the end of the year they had played 26 games in a row without a single victory. And still the end was not in sight.

When the 1945 football season got under way, America was at peace again. The Chicago-Pittsburgh merger was dissolved and the Cards were once again a "single" team, still coached by Phil Handler.

But the Cardinals started the new season the same way they'd ended the old one—with a defeat. This time they were shut out by the Lions after gaining only one first down all day. Another shutout followed at the hands of Cleveland, 21–0. In that game the Cards picked up only 25 yards rushing and never got past the Rams' 34.

By the time the Cards went up against Philadelphia for game three they had lost 28 in a row. They didn't beat the Eagles either, although they did manage to score their first points of the season. A partially blocked kick gave them possession on the Eagles' 38. Paul Christman, their new passer, kept firing until his team reached the 2, and then Frank Seno lugged the ball over. The kick for the extra point failed, and the Cards lost, 21–6.

The Cardinals' next game was against their home-town rivals, the Chicago Bears. The Bears had lost their first two games of the season and were hungry for their first win. The Cardinals didn't figure to do very much against them. Sure enough, the Bears jumped out in front in the first period, as quarterback Sid Luckman hit Kenny Kavanaugh on a 64-yard touchdown play.

But then the Cardinals struck back. Leo Cantor, a former New York Giant back, and Frank Seno, who came from the Redskins, alternated carrying the ball. Seno ripped off gains of 21 and 13 yards and Cantor went in from the 2, tying the game at 7–all.

Later in the game Cantor intercepted a Luckman pass on his own 15. Moments later Cantor threw a pass to end Ed Rucinski, good for 63 yards. Three plays later the Cards scored another touchdown to lead, 14–7.

The Cards scored once more on a fluke play. The Bears had the ball deep in their own territory, when

Luckman dropped back over his own goal line and tried to pass. The ball hit the crossbar and bounced out of the end zone. That scored as a two-point safety for the Cards.

The game ended with the Cardinals in front, 16–7. Finally, after 29 consecutive losses, the Cardinals had won a game! Their record-breaking losing streak was finally snapped. But that was to be their only victory of the season. The Cardinals lost their next six games and ended the schedule with a 1–9 record.

The following year Jimmy Conzelman returned to coach the Cardinals, and everything seemed to turn around for the team. Conzelman began the massive rebuilding job necessary to win, and in 1946 the Cardinals posted a 6–5 record. In 1947 they racked up a 9–3 season, then went on to defeat Philadelphia for the NFL championship. And in 1948 they won the Division crown with a total of eleven wins and just one loss.

The Chicago Cardinals had come all the way back. For two years they did not win a game, then for two more years they were rebuilt, and in the final two years they were the best in the West! In the years that followed, the NFL saw some pretty good teams—and some pretty bad ones. But for more than 30 years, no team even approached the Cardinals' incredible 29-game losing streak.

LIKE FATHER,
LIKE SON

Many fathers dream that their sons will follow in their footsteps. Usually, a successful lawyer wants his son to become a lawyer, a doctor hopes that his boy will also practice medicine, and an accountant thinks his profession is fine for his son.

Football players have that same dream, and very often it comes true. John McKay, head coach of the University of Southern California Trojans, had a fine receiver on his 1974 Rose Bowl team—his son, John McKay, Jr. One of Michigan's greatest running backs, Heisman Trophy winner Tommy Harmon, has watched approvingly as his son, Mark Harmon, played some fine football for UCLA. And Bobby Layne, one of pro football's greatest passers, has proudly followed the progress of his son, Alan Layne, a defensive back at Texas Christian University.

In the 1940s, a man named Dub Jones joined the Brooklyn Dodgers of the old All-America Football Conference. A great all-around player, he could carry the ball, catch passes, and even play in the defensive backfield. Dub later played with the Cleveland Browns and went on to become one of the finest halfbacks in the NFL when the Browns were admitted to the league. In a 1951 game against the Chicago Bears, Dub tied the scoring record by getting six touchdowns— four by rushing and two by catching touchdown passes.

A little more than two months before Dub Jones tied that record, his son Bert was born. At the age of two, Bert developed rickets and had to wear braces on his legs. A future in football seemed like an impossible dream for the young boy. Bert eventually recovered, but his illness left him pigeon-toed and bowlegged. Still, he could run as fast as most boys his age.

Even as a child, Bert was determined to follow in his father's footsteps. When he was in the first grade his teacher asked him what he wanted to be when he grew up.

"A pro football player," the youngster replied.

"But suppose you aren't good enough?"

"I'm going to be a pro football player," the boy insisted. "I don't want to be anything else."

Under the watchful eye of his father, Bert did develop his football skills. And after he graduated from high school, he went to Louisiana State University, just as his father had done. At LSU, Bert Jones became an All-America quarterback. In his senior year he threw 14 touchdown passes and was voted the team's Most Valuable Player. The Associated Press named him

Dub Jones gathers in a pass in 1961 . . .

Southeastern Conference "Back of the Week" three times. Overall, in his varsity career, Jones set 20 records and tied another. Most of those records had been set by another magnificent LSU passer named Y.A. Tittle, who later became a star quarterback for the Forty-Niners and the Giants in the NFL.

Jones closed his college career in a blaze of glory. He was the number one draft choice of the Baltimore

. . . and son Bert throws one some twelve years later.

Colts. Before reporting to training camp, he started in the College All-Star game and completed nine passes in 17 attempts for 79 yards against the great defense of the champion Miami Dolphins.

Playing for Baltimore in the 1973 pre-season exhibition games, Jones was a sensation. Against the Detroit Lions he hit on eleven out of 15 passes, including a touchdown pass. Late in the game the rookie passer engineered two sustained drives for touchdowns, which won the game.

Jones repeated that performance against Denver. This time he connected with twelve passes in 19 attempts for 130 yards, put together two late drives, and again was responsible for the game-winning score.

The Baltimore coaches couldn't have been happier with Jones' pre-season showing. Altogether, he had thrown 51 passes and completed 28 for a total of 244 yards. Two of the passes had gone for touchdowns. And, most important, he had been intercepted only once. When the regular season began, Jones was chosen as the Colts' starting quarterback, ahead of the more experienced Marty Domres.

But as soon as the season officially got under way, Jones ran into trouble. For the first half of the opener against Cleveland, he did well enough, throwing a touchdown pass to tie the game at 7–all. Then the Baltimore offense and defense fell apart, and Cleveland went on to win, 24–14.

Jones started the next four games, and the Colts lost three of them. Only a 14–9 victory over New Orleans saved them from a total wipeout.

Jones was benched for the sixth game, and Marty Domres started. Eager to show his ability, Domres led the Colts to a 29–27 victory over the Detroit Lions. Domres was outstanding, connecting with nine passes in 13 tries, including a 66-yard scoring pass to Glenn Doughty. For the rest of the season, Domres was the Colts' first-string quarterback, although Jones did see some action too. Baltimore never did get going and finished the season tied with the Jets for last place in the AFC's Eastern Division.

Nor was 1974 an improvement. Baltimore had little in the way of scoring punch and almost no blocking. In one game against Buffalo, Jones saw some action. He would have been better off on the bench. Late in the game he was sacked twice. The Baltimore passing attack gained exactly 1 yard, and the Colts were defeated 27–14.

The final game of the season matched the Colts against the New York Jets. By then, Baltimore was just playing out the schedule, having won only two and lost eleven. The Jets, on the other hand, were red hot. After a dismal beginning, Joe Namath had led the team to five straight wins. One more victory would give New York a 7 won, 7 lost record. General manager Weeb Ewbank would be retiring at season's end, and he was not about to finish his career as a loser.

Namath got the Jets off winging in the first period with a 25-yard touchdown pass to Jerome Barkum, but Jones got that back for Baltimore with a scoring pass to halfback Lydell Mitchell. Then New York began to run away with the game. Fullback John Riggins plunged for two touchdowns, and Burgess Owens ran 29 yards with an intercepted pass for the Jets' fourth touchdown of the half.

With just seconds to go in the half, the Colts tried to score again. Jones hit Bill Olds with a pass to put the Colts in field-goal distance. Marty Domres came in to hold the ball. But it was a fake. Domres picked up the ball, ran to his right, and threw to a receiver. But the pass was incomplete. On the next play the Colts went for the field goal and made it just before the clock ran out. Now Baltimore trailed, 28–10.

The game was hopelessly lost, and everyone seemed

to know it—everyone but Bert Jones. There was only one way to put the Colts back in the game, and that was by passing. So Jones took to the air. He got off three straight completions: to Mitchell for 5 yards, to Olds for 11, and to rookie receiver Freddie Scott for 39. Then he threw to Mitchell for 3 and to tight end Raymond Chester for the touchdown. The scoring drive had used up 2 minutes, 35 seconds; five good passes in a row, and Baltimore was back in business.

Namath fired right back. He forced Baltimore to tighten their defenses by using John Riggins on two line plays. Then, two quick passes gave the Jets another touchdown. Now the New Yorkers were leading, 35–17.

Then it was Jones' turn to throw the ball. A swing pass to rookie Roger Carr gained 7 yards. With the Jets expecting more passes, Jones crossed them up with a draw play, Mitchell carrying, and that went for 12 yards. Jones returned to the air route with four more passes, all on target. The Colt drive sputtered momentarily when Mitchell tried an end run and gained only 2 yards. But Jones went upstairs again. Three more completions to Don McCauley, Ray Chester, and Lydell Mitchell gave the Colts another TD. The third period ended with the Jets on top, 35–24.

Joe Namath realized that his team needed more points if they were to keep the lead. A long drive led to a field goal, making the score 38–24. Jones retaliated with three more passes in a row. Jones tried a fourth throw, but this time the Jets were ready and Owens intercepted.

The high-scoring game continued, and the Jets finally won it, 45–38. When the gun sounded to signal

Colt quarterback Bert Jones gets off one of his record-breaking passes against the New York Jets in 1974.

the end of the game—and the end of the season—Joe Namath walked slowly over to Bert Jones and shook his hand.

"Congratulations," said the winning passer.

"Thanks, Joe," said the loser.

Bert Jones may have lost the game, but he'd won something a lot more enduring—a place in the NFL record book. His 17 consecutive pass completions had set a brand new mark for quarterbacks.

So move over, Dub Jones. You merely *tied* a pro football record. Your son Bert has one record all to himself!

THE GLUE-FINGERED RECEIVER

Every football fan has heard the pet phrases used to describe different types of players. For instance, a good running back is called "hard charging" or "shifty," or "tough to bring down," while a good quarterback is said to "throw darts," "read the defenses," or "mix up his plays smartly."

And as everyone knows, a good receiver must be "glue-fingered," have "blazing speed," or know "all the right moves." Yet when Don Maynard broke into the NFL he could only have been described as "fumble-fingered." He certainly did not have blazing speed, and he had almost none of the moves required of a wide receiver. Of course, at that time he wasn't a receiver at all but a running back. Still, the record book clearly shows that in the years that followed he caught more passes for more yardage than any player in football history.

75

Jet receiver Don Maynard has trouble hanging on to the ball against a determined Roger Wehrli of the St. Louis Cardinals.

Maynard began his college career at Rice Institute but switched to Texas Western for his three varsity years. There he became one of the best running backs in the Southwest (he was also a pretty good defensive back). In his three years at Texas Western the team won 25 games and lost only five.

Maynard was the seventh draft choice of the New York Giants in 1958, and it was then that his troubles began. From the outset he was under great pressure. He had no chance to make the starting line-up as a running back because the Giants were already set there with the great Alex Webster and Frank Gifford. So Maynard was used as a sub or on the special teams.

Even when he did get a chance to play, Maynard was hardly impressive. In one exhibition game, the nervous rookie fumbled three times. He managed to recover the ball twice, but the damage to his reputation was already done. The pressure on Maynard mounted when the regular season began and he fumbled a punt in an important game against the Cleveland Browns. The fans booed him mercilessly.

Unfortunately, Maynard's problems weren't restricted to his hands. His footwork was also criticized. Maynard had an unusual, loping running style. It seemed that he covered more turf in one stride than other runners covered in two. But coach Allie Sherman insisted he change.

"Shorten your stride," Sherman told Maynard. "This isn't a track meet."

To top it all off, the Giant staff even objected to the rookie's personal appearance. In 1958 the closely cropped crew cut was the popular hair style. Yet Maynard had long sideburns and refused to trim them.

It seemed that nothing about Maynard pleased the Giants. In his first season he caught only five passes for a total of 84 yards. So it came as no surprise when the Giants cut him before the 1959 schedule began.

No other NFL team showed any interest in the young running back, so Maynard joined the Hamilton Tiger Cats of the Canadian Football League. But he didn't last long there, either. Late in the '59 season, the Tiger Cats decided they needed a player who could double on the offensive and defensive teams. Maynard was considered too light, and Hamilton found a suitable player in the United States. Unfortunately, only a certain number of Americans were allowed to play on any team in the Canadian League, and the new player put Hamilton over the quota. As a result, Maynard was dropped. For the second time in two years, it seemed that his pro football career was ended.

And then in 1960 the American Football League was organized. Because he was a Texan by birth, Maynard tried to hook on with the Dallas Texans (later to become the Kansas City Chiefs), but they weren't interested. He also wrote to the New York Titans (who later became the New York Jets). Titan coach Sammy Baugh, also born in Texas, invited Maynard to the New York camp for a tryout.

Baugh decided that the 175-pound Maynard was too light to be a really good running back, but he saw something in Maynard that no one else had noticed. Maynard still wasn't "blazing fast," but he *was* quick and agile. He wasn't the greatest blocker in the world, but he wasn't bad. In short, Baugh reasoned, Don Maynard might be converted into a successful receiver.

Before Maynard could become a wide receiver,

however, he had to learn to think like one. Like many running backs, Maynard knew the simple pass cuts: the sideline, the buttonhook, the long-and-deep. But Maynard didn't have the fakes, the moves, needed by receivers. In his attempts to shake free, he often broke the Titans' patterns. He was like a young kid, running around in circles, calling out, "Hey, Butch, throw it to me, I'm in the clear." Half the time his quarterback wasn't sure where to find him in a crowd. It was often a toss-up as to who would find Maynard first—the Titan quarterback or the opposing team's defense.

Still, Maynard did manage to shake the defenses quite often—and the quarterbacks found him often enough. In 1960, he caught 72 passes, good for 1,265 yards and six touchdowns. Maynard was definitely looking better as a receiver than he had as a back, but he still seemed an unlikely candidate for superstardom. His fumbling continued to be a problem. And, of course, in those early years the AFL defenses were considered very weak.

Hampering Maynard's development as a receiver was the Titans' lack of a solid quarterback. It helps a lot when a passer and receiver work together for a long time, and each knows the other's strong points, the timing, the right time to throw each particular kind of pass. With the Titans, the quarterback show was like a revolving door, with the passers coming and going. As soon as Maynard could adjust to one quarterback, the Titans would come up with another. Al Dorow, Dick Jamieson, Johnny Green, Lee Grosscup, Ed Songin, Harold Stephens, and Dick Wood were some of the passers Maynard had to work with.

In one 1960 game Dorow started but was sacked

behind the line and suffered a rib injury. His replacement, Dick Jamieson, was also hurt, so Dorow had to return to the line-up. Finally, the Titans put in a quarterback named Bob Scrabis, who had been a second-stringer at Penn State. Needless to say, it was a long, hard game for Maynard.

But as the years passed Maynard gained experience. He learned the moves and stopped running around aimlessly in the defensive backfield. And a new spirit came to the team in 1963, when the franchise was sold to Sonny Werblin. He changed the name of the club to the Jets. Then he began looking for the quarterback who could weld the team together, make it move. In 1965 Werblin found his man playing for the University of Alabama: Joe Willie Namath.

When Namath broke into the Jets' starting line-up for good, he had several fine receivers waiting to take his throws, including George Sauer, Pete Lammons, Bake Turner, and, of course, Don Maynard. He threw to all of them, but when he needed the big gain his target was usually Maynard.

In 1965 Maynard caught 68 passes for 1,218 yards, an average of 17.9 per catch. The next year he gathered in 48 tosses for 840 yards and 17.5 yards per catch. In 1967 Maynard received 71 passes for 1,434 yards and 20.2 yards per catch. It wasn't that Namath always threw the long bomb toward his flanker; rather it was Maynard's ability to run with the ball once he grabbed it that accounted for his great yardage.

Maynard opened the 1968 season as the leading receiver in the AFL. Ahead of him were three NFL receivers: Ray Berry, Billy Howton, and Tommy McDonald. By the time the year ended there was

Maynard is congratulated by teammate Joe Namath after the Jets defeated Oakland for the 1968 American Football League championship.

nobody ahead of him in yardage gained. He amassed 1,297 yards for a total of 9,445. Since all the others were retired, he was top man in that department.

But Ray Berry, who had been the favorite receiver of the great Johnny Unitas, still held the record for total receptions with 631. Maynard (with 604) was far behind, and time was running out for the 31-year-old receiver.

Maynard was now a step slower than before, but he had vast experience. He had been up against most of the league's defensive backs many times and knew what to expect of them. In 1970 he caught 31 passes,

Maynard is knocked off his feet during a 1968 game, but the "glue-fingered" receiver keeps a firm grip on the ball.

adding 525 yards to his all-time total, and the next year he grabbed 21 more for 408 yards. He had his injuries, the bad days when he couldn't play. But slowly Raymond Berry's mark came into reach. The 1971 season ended with Maynard only 27 receptions away from the record.

As the 1972 season got under way, many observers thought it would be Maynard's last real opportunity to overtake Berry. Maynard was now over 35 years of age.

When he was tackled hard, he got up more slowly. Namath didn't throw to him as often as before, and Maynard was spending more time on the bench in favor of younger receivers. But as long as he was in there, Maynard was still a threat. Game by game, pass by pass, he inched up on Berry's record.

By December 11, 1972, Maynard was just seven receptions away from a new all-time record. That day, the Jets played their bitter rivals, the Oakland Raiders. Namath decided to give his buddy every possible chance. But the Raiders were waiting for Maynard. After one catch Maynard got up with an ugly bruise on his cheekbone. Finally, late in the game, Namath delivered a bullet right into Maynard's hands and the old pro held onto the ball. It was the seventh pass he had caught in the game. The referee called time and the ball was thrown out, to be given to the veteran flanker.

With that, his 632nd reception, Don Maynard moved ahead of Ray Berry and every other receiver in the NFL record book. He added one more catch to his lifetime record before the season ended, giving him a grand total of 633 receptions for 11,834 yards. But there is no sentiment in pro football. Before the 1973 season the Jets dropped Maynard to make room for the younger, faster receivers coming up. Maynard managed to catch on with the St. Louis Cardinals, but was released almost immediately from that team, too.

For the third time in 15 years, Maynard's career seemed to be over. This time, however, it was really for keeps. Don Maynard would never catch another pass, but his outstanding achievements would remain in the record books for years to come.

THE
LONGEST
DAY

On December 25, 1971, the Kansas City Chiefs were slated to play the Miami Dolphins in an American Football Conference playoff game. According to the records, the teams were evenly matched. Both had finished the regular season with identical 10–3–1 marks.

Nevertheless, the Chiefs were odds-on favorites to win—and with good reason. Over the years, Kansas City and Miami had met six times in regular season play; and each time, Kansas City had triumphed. In addition, Kansas City quarterback Len Dawson was an old pro, and, after two Super Bowl appearances, he knew how to keep cool under pressure. To top it all off, the Chiefs would be playing the playoff game before their hometown fans, which was bound to give them a great psychological advantage. According to the experts, Kansas City couldn't lose.

Die-hard Dolphin fans refused to be discouraged, however. They had their own idea about the game's outcome. And they figured Miami to win. In 14 regular season games, Miami had scored 315 points, while Kansas City had racked up 302 points. Thus, on offense, the Dolphins had averaged one point per game more than the Chiefs. Defensively, the Dolphins had yielded 174 points while the Chiefs had allowed 208. That meant that Miami had permitted $2\frac{1}{2}$ points per game less than Kansas City. Therefore, Miami fans claimed that the Dolphins were about $3\frac{1}{2}$ points better than the Chiefs. The Dolphins should win the game by a field goal.

It was an interesting theory, but it seemed more like wishful thinking than fact as the contest began. Kansas City's Jan Stenerud kicked off to Miami to open the game. But the Dolphins couldn't move the ball in their first series of plays and had to punt. The Chiefs took over in fine field position on their own 43, and Dawson began to move the team steadily. A screen pass to running back Ed Podolak gained 5, and then Wendell Hayes, the other K.C. running back, broke through the middle for 16. It wasn't all that easy, however. Dawson got good protection when he dropped back to pass, but his receivers just couldn't seem to hold onto the ball. Two of Dawson's passes went right through the hands of the intended receivers. Finally, Jan Stenerud, Kansas City's Norwegian-born place kicker, came in to try a 24-yard field goal. His kick cleared the bar with room to spare, and Kansas City went ahead, 3–0.

During most of the first quarter, Miami's inexperience and overeagerness were painfully apparent. On one series of plays the Chiefs were faced with a third down and just over 5 yards to go. Dawson's pass to Otis Taylor was incomplete, but Miami cornerback Curtis Johnson was offside. The penalty left Kansas City with a third-and-inches situation, and the Chiefs easily got the first down. On the next play, they ran the same screen pass that had hurt Miami earlier in the game. This time, Podolak scored, and now the Chiefs led, 10–0.

The Dolphins finally got going late in the period. Quarterback Bob Griese connected with wide receiver Paul Warfield for 35. Then he hit tight end Marv Fleming, bringing the ball to the Kansas City 4. A pass interference call put the ball on the 1, and big Larry Csonka bulled his way over the last chalk stripe to give the Dolphins their first touchdown of the day.

The Dolphins seemed to gain confidence as the game continued, and soon it was the Chiefs who were making the key mistakes. Twice they mounted good drives, but both times they failed to go all the way. Once a pass intended for Taylor was intercepted by Curtis Johnson on the Dolphins' 10-yard line. Later, a good gain by workhorse Ed Podolak was called back because the Chiefs were caught clipping.

Once more, Stenerud came out to try a field goal, this one from 29 yards out. It looked like a certain 3-pointer. Stenerud was considered the best place kicker in the conference, and from inside the 35-yard line he was deadly. But now Stenerud's kick went wide to the right, and he trotted off the field shaking his head, unable to believe he had missed such an easy shot.

The experienced Chiefs kept making mistakes, and the green Dolphins kept capitalizing on them. Late in

Miami's Larry Csonka barrels into the end zone for a Dolphin touchdown in the 1971 AFL playoffs against the Kansas City Chiefs.

the second quarter, the Chiefs had possession deep in their own territory. All they had to do was run out the clock and then go into the dressing room with a 10–7 halftime lead. But the usually reliable Ed Podolak fumbled, and Miami recovered on the Kansas City 12. Griese advanced the ball to the 5-yard line with a pass to Warfield. The Chiefs braced and knocked down two more of his passes, so Garo Yepremian, Miami's little left-footed kicker, booted the field goal to tie up the game at 10–all.

Kansas City coach Hank Stram must have given his players quite a pep talk during the intermission. For when the teams took the field for the second half, Len Dawson and the Chiefs showed the Dolphins how championship football should be played. They gave a textbook demonstration of ball control, and Miami was all but helpless.

The first play, a pass out in the flat, lost a yard, but after that the Chiefs began to grind out the first downs. Dawson passed to Elmo Wright for 17 yards, Hayes hit through tackle for 7, and Dawson completed two straight passes to Taylor for a total of 9 more. One outstanding play, a forward-lateral, from Dawson to Taylor to Podolak, covered 39 yards, but the gain was washed out on a clipping penalty. Still Kansas City kept pounding away, firing off the ball, shoving back the fine Miami defensive line again and again. When the Chiefs got to the Miami 13, Jim Otis tried a line smash and was almost stopped for no gain. But Otis made a terrific second effort, crashing through to the 1. And on the next play he took it over.

That Kansas City drive had used up 9 minutes, 44 seconds of the third period. It had taken the Chiefs 17 plays to score the touchdown. But Bob Griese got the score back for Miami in a couple of minutes, with only a few plays. He covered most of the ground with a pair of beautifully executed passes, one to receiver Howard Twilley, the other to Paul Warfield. Each toss gained 23 yards. Then, from inside the 1, Jim Kiick slammed into the end zone to tie the score, 17–all.

After that, both teams settled down to a war of

nerves, pushing and shoving each other back and forth over the length of the gridiron. Under pressure, both teams made heartbreaking mistakes. One Kansas City drive faltered when Wendell Hayes fumbled. Then Griese threw an interception deep in Chiefs territory.

The seasoned veteran, Len Dawson, finally made a breakthrough with one big play. With the ball on his own 34, the Kansas City passer spotted Elmo Wright behind the safety and hit him with a perfect pass. Wright tucked the ball under his arm and streaked for pay dirt. He was hauled down just short of the goal line. Desperately, he tried to crawl into the end zone, but the officials brought the ball back. On the next play Podolak swept right, picked up a great block by Wendell Hayes, and scored. That put the Chiefs back in front, 24–17.

With time running out, Griese began throwing his darts and finding open receivers. Five times his passes fell into friendly hands. The fifth one was a 5-yarder to Marv Fleming for the TD. Then, with just 1 minute, 36 seconds left to play, Yepremian came in and kicked the extra point that tied the game again.

Seconds later, the Kansas City fans were on their feet, screaming. Ed Podolak took the kickoff on his own goal line and streaked away, picking up key blocks, and breaking into the clear. He made it all the way to Miami's 22 before being stopped.

Now the Chiefs seemed to have the game locked up. All they had to do was hang onto the ball and stay in field goal position. So Dawson kept the ball on the ground, with Podolak carrying. In three plays he lost a total of 2 yards, but that didn't matter. The Chiefs still had possession. With 31 seconds to go, Jan Stenerud,

Ed Podolak (14) picks up a few yards for the Chiefs before being brought down by the Miami defense.

the AFC's all-star place kicker, jogged out to practice his specialty.

The ball was spotted down on the Miami 31. Stenerud stepped forward and booted. From where he was standing on the sidelines, Kansas City coach Hank Stram thought the kick was good, but the referee signaled that the ball had gone wide to the right. Stenerud walked sadly off the field. He had squandered the chance to win for the Chiefs. Miami took possession on the 20, and seconds later the gun sounded to signal the end of regulation play.

Unlike regular season contests, a championship game cannot end in a tie. So for the fourth time in NFL history, a post-season game went into sudden-death overtime. Len Dawson won the flip of the coin, and the Chiefs chose to receive the kickoff to begin the fifth period. Once more, Ed Podolak brought the crowd to its feet as he returned the ball to the Chiefs' 46.

It was almost a replay of the first period. Len Dawson tried the screen pass right, with Podolak as his receiver, and it went for 8 yards. Hayes made 4 over tackle. But the K.C. drive bogged down on Miami's 35.

Stenerud had been hit by bad luck so far. He had already missed two easy field goals—and either of those would have won the game for the Chiefs in regulation time. Now he'd be making an attempt from the 42, which was well within his range. But it just wasn't his day. The pass from center was a little high, and by the time the ball was placed down, a charging Miami linebacker, Nick Buoniconti, had slipped through the line to block the kick. All season long, Stenerud had been a league leader in field goals, making 26 out of 44 attempts. But now, when the pressure was really on, he'd missed three out of four.

For the rest of the period the action seesawed across the field, with neither team penetrating into scoring territory. Garo Yepremian tried a field goal from his own 48, but it fell short. The fifth period ended as it had begun—with the teams deadlocked, 24–24.

The sixth period started slowly. Then, with 3 minutes gone, the Dolphins got possession on their own 30. Jim Kiick went around left end for 5. And then came the game-breaker.

In the huddle, Griese called for Miami's "roll trap right" play. It called for Kiick and Griese to start toward the strong side. The handoff would go to Csonka, who would have the two guards running interference for him in the other direction. As planned, Csonka thundered through left tackle and powered his way for 29 yards, all the way to the Chiefs' 36.

Now the Dolphins were in field goal range. But they tried to work the ball in closer to give Yepremian an easier shot. Kiick plunged for 2 yards, Csonka for 4, and then Kiick was stopped at the 30-yard line for no gain.

All afternoon Garo Yepremian had watched Stenerud's kicks go wide. Now it was the Miami kicker's turn to show what he could do. The ball was spotted on the 37 with Karl Noonan holding. All eyes were on Yepremian as he stepped into the ball. Garo's kick went up and cleared the crossbar. Exhausted and dejected, the Kansas City Chiefs walked slowly off the field, while the jubilant Dolphins surrounded their place kicker. The longest game in NFL history had finally ended with Miami on top, 27–24.

The record-breaking game had lasted 82 minutes, 40

Miami kicker Garo Yepremian ends the stalemate with the game-winning field goal in the sixth period.

seconds, or slightly more than five and a half quarters. The old mark of 77 minutes, 54 seconds had been set by the Dallas Texans in 1962. Oddly enough, the Texans had moved to Kansas City in 1963, where they were renamed the Chiefs. So actually, the Chiefs had broken their own record. And Len Dawson had been the quarterback in both long games.

There was one more strange coincidence. Those who put their faith in experience and the hometown advantage were wrong. Those who had predicted the game according to cold statistics were exactly right. The Dolphins won the game by the margin of a field goal. Of course, it took them a lot longer than anyone expected.

THE
HALF-FOOTED
KICKER

In the early 1900s the Chicago Cubs signed a young pitcher named Mordecai "Three Finger" Brown. The rookie earned his nickname honestly. As a result of a farm accident during his youth, Brown had only three useful fingers on his pitching hand. He had lost the index finger, and the one next to it had been badly mangled. Yet Three Finger Brown became a fantastic pitcher.

Brown actually made his handicap work for him. Most pitchers grip the ball with three fingers, anyway, and because of Brown's unusual grip, his tosses seemed to have a natural sinking-curving path to the plate. Brown perfected his unorthodox pitches, and even the best hitters in the league found him hard to beat.

Another athlete who refused to be stopped by a handicap was football's Tom Dempsey. Although he was born with only one hand and only half of his right foot, Dempsey kicked his way right into the NFL record book.

Tom's parents never treated him like an invalid, and as a result he never felt like one. Instead of feeling sorry for himself, Tom went out and competed with other boys.

Because he was so active as a boy, the rest of Tom's body grew straight and hard. He was broad-shouldered and strong. In athletics, only his foot gave him trouble. He had to stuff wads of toilet paper into his right shoe.

By the time Dempsey enrolled at Palomar (California) Junior College, he had earned quite a reputation in sports. He was on the wrestling team, threw the shot in track, and played defensive end on the football team. Strange as it seems, his specialty was kicking field goals—barefoot! The only protection for the foot was a strip or two of tape. His powerful leg would send the stump of a foot crashing into the football, which would sail away in a high, on-target arc.

Pro football is a bruising, head-banging game, tough enough for anyone with all his feet and hands, let alone a man like Tom Dempsey who was minus a hand and half his kicking foot. Yet Dempsey was determined to make a career in the game. After graduation, he received a tryout with the San Diego Chargers of the American Football League. The coaches watched in awe as he sent his tape-covered stump banging into the football. Time after time, from every angle and from all distances, he booted the ball cleanly through the goalposts. Head coach Sid Gillman saw the booming kicks and predicted—only half-jokingly—that someday Dempsey might kick a 90-yard field goal.

Dempsey was placed on the San Diego taxi squad, waiting to be called up to the team. Gillman had a special shoe designed for the would-be kicker, but it didn't work. It was made of fiberglass and was shaped like a normal shoe, but it was too heavy and hurt his foot.

Dempsey decided to design his own kicking shoe. He wanted one that had no aluminum bars or other type of protection. It had to be shaped like his own foot and, most important of all, it had to be comfortable. He found a shoemaker who was willing to work with him, and together they worked on the shape and feel of the shoe. It was not an easy job. Every time the shoemaker put a shoe together, Dempsey would try it out, then come back with new suggestions for changing it.

There were two good results from all this labor. First of all, after much trial and error Dempsey finally got the type of shoe he wanted. And as an added bonus, Dempsey put in so much extra practice time trying out the shoe that his kicks became longer and even more accurate.

Dempsey never did get a chance to kick for the Chargers, and they eventually dropped him. Then he tried out with the New Orleans Saints. The Saints already had a field-goal kicker named Charlie Durkee, but in 1969 Dempsey beat him out for the job.

Around the league Dempsey was considered a pretty good kicker. But the Saints didn't have much of a team, especially during the 1970 season. By the time the season was half over, the Saints had won one, lost six, and tied one. Dempsey's record wasn't much better. In his first seven games he had made only five of fifteen field-goal attempts.

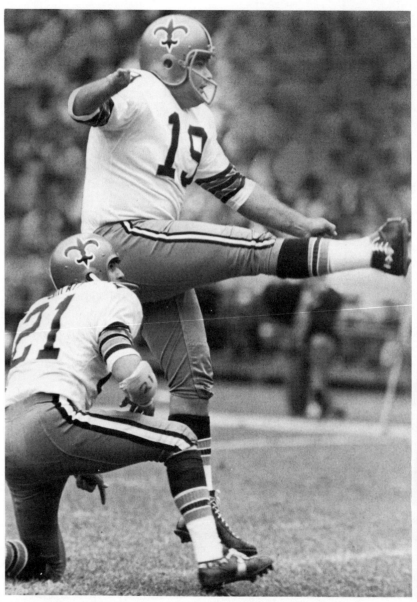

Tom Dempsey gets off a big kick for the New Orleans Saints in 1970.

The Saints' eighth game of the season, on November 8, didn't figure to improve their standing. On that day, they would be facing the Detroit Lions, one of the strongest teams in the league. The Lions seemed a sure bet to devour the slumping Saints.

When the game began, however, the Lions didn't look nearly as fierce as usual. It seemed that every time they got within scoring distance they would commit a turnover. Unfortunately, the Saints didn't take advantage of the Lions' weakness. In fact, the only scoring punch they could muster in the first quarter was a 29-yard field goal by Tom Dempsey, which gave them a slim 3–0 lead.

The Lions came back with two touchdowns in the next two periods, but Dempsey kept the Saints in the game with a pair of field goals. The Lions led, 14–9, going into the last period. So far, Dempsey had been responsible for every single point on New Orleans' side of the scoreboard.

Then in the fourth quarter New Orleans linebacker Jackie Burkett intercepted a pass by Detroit quarterback Bill Munson and returned it to the Lion 34. Eight plays took the Saints to the Detroit 4-yard line, and then running back Tom Barrington carried the ball over for a touchdown. Then Dempsey booted the ball over the crossbar for the extra point, and the Saints reclaimed the lead, 16–14.

The Lions came roaring back, with quarterback Greg Landry leading a strategic attack, eating up time as the ball was pushed relentlessly toward the New Orleans goal. With only 14 seconds left, Errol Mann kicked an 18-yard field goal to put Detroit back into the lead, 17–16.

Mann's kick had taken 3 seconds, so that left the Saints with only 11 seconds to save the game.

Al Dodd of New Orleans took the kickoff on his 14 and added 14 yards more on the runback. Another 3 seconds were gone on that play. Only 8 seconds were left. Then New Orleans passer Billy Kilmer hit receiver Al Dodd with a crisp 17-yard heave, and Dodd stepped out of bounds to stop the clock. Still, the play had consumed another 6 precious seconds. Only 2 more ticks of the clock remained.

New Orleans coach J. D. Roberts was faced with a crucial decision. He had two choices, both incredible longshots. The ball was just across the Saints' 45-yard line, and there was barely enough time for one more play. He could send quarterback Kilmer in to try for the winning TD. But he knew the Lions would go into a prevent defense, filling the field with defensive backs. Kilmer might be able to complete a short pass, but a touchdown toss seemed an impossible dream.

Roberts' only other alternative was to send in Tom Dempsey for the field goal attempt—another seemingly impossible dream. The ball would be spotted back on the New Orleans 37-yard line—63 yards away from the goalposts. In the entire history of NFL history, no one had ever made a field goal from that far out. The longest recorded kick was a 56-yarder by Bert Rechichar in 1953—and that hadn't even been threatened in 17 years.

The odds were against it, but Roberts decided to gamble on the field goal. Joe Scarpati knelt at the 37 to hold the ball. Dempsey took one step and swung his right leg in a short, powerful arc. The ball soared high into the air, hurtled end-over-end across the vast

Demsey checks out some of his special shoes before suiting up.

distance, then finally tumbled down—just barely clearing the crossbar. The referee threw up his arms to signal the kick was good.

The crowd of 66,910 fans exploded into cheers, while the Detroit defenders shuffled off the field, shaking their heads in disbelief. Dempsey's incredible kick of 63 yards, the longest in NFL history, had given the Saints a last-second, upset victory.

There were a great many comments after that historic kick. Billy Kilmer, the Saints' quarterback, raved, "The man just kicked himself into the Hall of Fame . . . that's all he did." One football official called Dempsey's foot a "sledgehammer." When asked for his reaction, Detroit defenseman Alex Karras just shook his head. He still couldn't believe the amazing feat he'd just witnessed. Finally he quipped, "I think Tom Dempsey was confused. When the ball is spotted down on the 37-yard line, the kicker is supposed to aim for the nearest goalposts—not the ones farthest away!"

PITY
THE POOR
PASSERS

A group of pro football statisticians once decided to find out how long it takes to execute a pass play. They wanted to determine the *exact* time, from the instant the quarterback took the ball from center, dropped back, and located his receiver, to the time he actually fired away. After much work with stop watches, examining films of many games, they all agreed that, on the average, the whole play took 3½ seconds.

There are three ways of looking at those 3½ seconds. To the harassed passer, who knows he must get rid of the ball before he can count to four, they rarely seem enough. To his blockers, who are trying to hold off the charge by defensive linemen and linebackers, the fleeting seconds seem like an eternity. But to the opposing defenders, who must stop the passer, 3½ seconds can be just enough time to do the job.

When a pass clicks, the quarterback gets most of the credit. When it doesn't work, his blockers are often blamed. But in reality, the success or failure of a pass play almost always depends on the enemy defense. Even the greatest passer will have trouble if he can't find an open receiver.

For example, take Jim Hardy, a fine quarterback who played for the old Chicago Cardinals. On September 24, 1950, Hardy came up against the Philadelphia Eagles. The Eagle defense played one of its best games ever—and Hardy experienced one of the worst days on record. He attempted 39 passes and completed only twelve. Eight of his passes were intercepted, and several of those resulted in Eagle touchdowns.

November 15, 1964, was just as demoralizing for Len Dawson, quarterback of the Kansas City Chiefs. The San Diego defense was so effective that day that Dawson fumbled seven times, an NFL record.

But such misfortunes are rare in a passer's career. Much of the time his blocking holds up, and a receiver gets into the clear momentarily. A good passer will complete about half of his attempts and gain good yardage. As a rule, the 3½ seconds is enough time—unless, of course, the opposing team has a truly great defense.

The 1967 Oakland Raider defense was one of the best in the history of professional football. They specialized in knifing through the line, getting by the pass pocket, and sacking the quarterback. Game after game, they made life miserable for opposing passers. Long after the season was over, rival coaches were still trying to figure out what made the Oakland defense so effective.

For example, why was defensive end Ben Davidson so tough? Davidson hadn't even been a first stringer at the University of Washington, where he played college ball. He was drafted far down on the list by the New York Giants in 1961, but was sent to the Packers before the season started. In Green Bay, Davidson sat on the bench for a season and was finally traded to Washington. With the Redskins, he was just so-so—good one game, terrible the next. Finally, Washington gave up on the 6-foot-8, 275-pound lineman; and so did the rest of the NFL. Davidson was waived out of the league. But he caught on with Oakland in the American Football League in '64, and there he began to develop his full potential.

The Raiders' other defensive end was Isaac Lassiter, whose early career resembled Davidson's. Very few scouts had noticed him at tiny St. Augustine College in North Carolina, although at 6-foot-5 and 275 pounds he should have stood out like an elephant in a field of grass. The Rams signed Lassiter in 1962 but dropped him after three weeks. Then he played with Denver for a while, but the Broncos also released him. Part of his problem was his weight. Lassiter thought a defensive lineman had to be really big, and he ate himself up the scale to a point near the 300-pound mark. Oakland finally gave him a trial, burned the fat off his frame, and made him a starter.

At defensive tackle, Oakland had 6-foot-4, 260-pound Dan Birdwell from the University of Houston. When Birdwell first joined the Raiders in '62, they didn't know what to do with him. In college he had played center and guard on offense and linebacker on defense. But he kept getting bigger with each passing season, and finally the Raiders installed him at defensive tackle.

Birdwell had two things going for him. First, his hands were unbelievably large. He wore a size 17 ring—a 25-cent piece could slip through the ring quite easily. Second, he was fantastically strong. Birdwell was the kind of man who could hurt people unintentionally with a friendly slap on the back or a bone-crushing handshake. Any passer who saw the big tackle lumbering toward him—in a most *un*friendly manner —was bound to feel intimidated.

Oakland's other tackle was Tom Keating, a former All–Big Ten tackle from Michigan. Keating had been the fifth draft choice of the Kansas City Chiefs in 1964, but they traded him to Buffalo ten minutes after they got him. Keating injured his ankle during his first year with the Bills. The next year he hurt his left knee. Wary of a player who had two injuries in two years, Buffalo then traded him to Oakland. At 6-foot-2 and 247 pounds, he was the smallest and lightest of the Oakland front four, but his drive and determination made him one of the team's leaders.

The other Raider defenders were Gus Otto, Bill Budness, Dan Conners, Bill Laskey, and Carleton Oats. They were all good, solid players, but there wasn't a real superstar among them. Yet, working together, they made up an awesome defensive team.

The Denver Broncos were the first team to feel the Raiders' wrath in 1967. On September 10, they visited

The Raider front four (Ben Davidson, Tom Keating, Dan Birdwell, and Ike Lassiter) is an intimidating sight even in practice.

Oakland for the season's opener. The poor Broncs never did figure out what hit them. The game was like a nightmare, except that everyone was awake and it was dreadfully real.

The Oakland defense kept breaking in, forcing quarterback Steve Tensi into hurried passes. Gus Otto, the Raiders' 6-foot-1, 200-pound linebacker, was the first to make his presence known. Early in the game, he chased Tensi down and flattened him for an 18-yard loss. Tensi fumbled, and Otto recovered the ball. Later, Tom Keating grabbed Tensi for a loss of 8. Then

Bill Laskey caught the quarterback for a loss of 10.

In the third quarter, Tensi sat down for a much-needed rest and was replaced by Scotty Glacken. Birdwell got his big hands on the substitute quarterback and dumped him for a loss of 11. A while later, the whole front line knocked Glacken down for a loss of 9 more yards.

Tensi came back in the fourth quarter and took some more punishment. Birdwell grabbed him for a 10-yard loss, and then the whole forward wall sat on him for a 4-yard loss.

The Raiders romped to a 51–0 victory. And the Broncos wound up with a total of *minus* 53 yards in passing!

The Raiders' next victims were the Boston Patriots. Veteran quarterback Babe Parilli managed to escape the Oakland defenders for the first half, but then his luck ran out. Early in the third period, Ben Davidson got to Parilli and knocked him down for a 13-yard loss. On the very next play Davidson was there again, and this time Parilli was pushed back 11 yards. Later in the quarter, Gus Otto got into the action. The first time he hit Parilli, the loss was 8 yards. The second time it was only 7 yards, but Parilli fumbled and Dan Conners recovered for Oakland.

Parilli had had enough for a while, so Johnny Huarte came in to pass—at least he *tried* to pass. But Gus Otto took him down, too. Then Parilli came back in and was dropped twice more.

Len Dawson of Kansas City was the next passer to get his lumps from the Raiders. Once Otto hit him for a loss of 10, and later, Ike Lassiter piled into Dawson so hard that he fumbled. Dan Conners picked up the ball

Pressured by the rough and ready Oakland defenders, Denver quarterback Steve Tensi bobbles the ball.

and returned it 49 yards. That fumble led to a field goal, which turned out to be the winning margin as Oakland won a squeaker, 23–21.

Oakland finally lost a game to the New York Jets, mostly because Joe Namath was caught only twice, once each by Conners and Keating.

But in their next game, against the Buffalo Bills, the Raiders were rougher than ever. Quarterback Jack Kemp had to run for his life on almost every play. In the first quarter he was dropped by Davidson and then by Budness. In the second period Keating got to him first, and then Birdwell and Lassiter sacked him on successive plays. In the second half, Lassiter brought him down four times. Altogether, Kemp was thrown for losses totaling 79 yards.

The following week the Raider defenders seemed to be playing in San Diego's backfield. Deep in his own territory, San Diego quarterback John Hadl tried a pitchout to running back Dick Post behind the line of scrimmage. Dan Birdwell tore in and nailed Post behind the goal line for a safety. On another play, Post tried the option pass, but he never got the toss off; Ike Lassiter grabbed him for a loss of 9. Oats captured Hadl for a loss of 15 on another play, and Birdwell completed the action on sub quarterback Kay Stephenson for a 7-yard loss.

Steve Tensi of Denver had already tasted the Oakland defensive power, and in their second meeting the Raiders gave him another helping of the same thing. In the first period he was hit by Conners and Lassiter for a combined loss of 21 yards. In the second period Conners got to him again. Then, on two straight plays, Tensi was dropped for losses, first by Birdwell and Keating, then by Dan Conners. Jim Leclair took Tensi's place with no better luck. The substitute quarterback was creamed by Birdwell twice, by Davidson once, and by Lassiter once.

The carnage continued against Miami. Birdwell

sacked Bob Griese twice. On another play, Griese tried to get away with a quarterback keeper play and lost 6 more yards.

By that time the Raiders had won all but one game. Rival coaches were trying desperately to figure out a way to keep the Oakland line and linebackers away from their poor quarterbacks. But nothing seemed to work.

Lenny Dawson had another bad day against Oakland. He was dropped no less than six times. In the second period first Birdwell and then Keating and Davidson reached him on two straight plays for a combined loss of 20 yards. When they weren't actually sacking Dawson, the Oakland front four did an incredible job of intimidating him. The Kansas City passer was so eager to get rid of the ball that he made one mistake after another. Oakland defensive backs Warren Powers and Willie Brown each intercepted two passes, and one of the bad tosses was run back for a Raider touchdown.

And so the 1967 season went, game after game. Pete Beatherd of Houston found out what it was like to face the Oakland line, and Joe Namath was dropped again in the second meeting between the Raiders and Jets. No quarterback in the AFL was safe from the rough and ready Raiders.

Oakland's final game of the season, against Buffalo, was another massacre. In the second quarter Lassiter and Gus Otto crunched quarterback Jack Kemp for a loss of 3 yards, then Birdwell got to him for 7. In the third quarter Kemp tried to run away from Otto—in the wrong direction—and lost 15. Then Kemp was

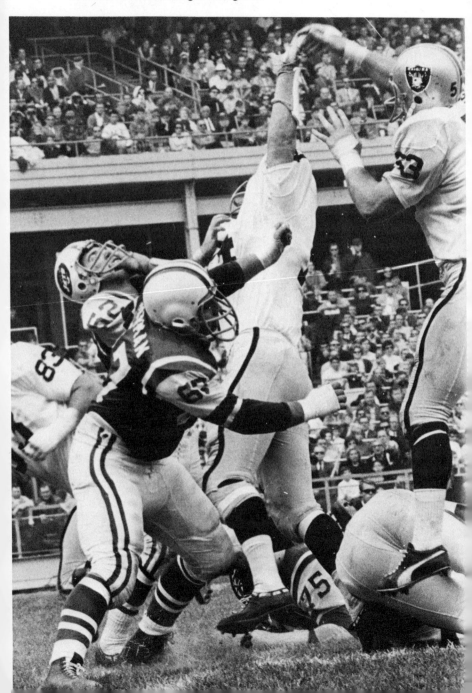

Oakland's Tom Keating shoves his hand under the face mask of New York's Al Atkinson during a 1967 game.

dumped by Carleton Oats for 4 more. Finally, Ben Davidson came charging after him, and Kemp fumbled. It would have been a loss of 14 yards, except that Oats picked up the football and ran it into the end zone for a Raider touchdown.

Oakland finished the season with a 13–1 record. The very best passers in the league had been powerless against the big Raider line. In 1966, the great "Doomsday Defense" of the Dallas Cowboys had set a record by sacking opposing quarterbacks 66 times. But now the Oakland Raiders had broken that record, dumping the poor passer 67 times. And they did it with a group of "pretty good" individual players, who were welded into a *team*—one of the finest defenses ever to step onto a football field.

JOHNNY U: MISTER QUARTERBACK

This is a book about record-breakers, the teams and individuals with the best statistics in various categories. But there are some achievements which can never be measured by mere numbers. For example, one clutch play that wins a ballgame is worth four spectacular plays that have little bearing on the outcome of a game. Similarly, one leader who molds his players into a winning team is worth a whole line-up of individual stars who worry only about their own personal glory.

So when Johnny Unitas retired after the end of the 1973 season, he was admired and respected by every professional player in the NFL. During his outstanding career with the Baltimore Colts, Unitas amassed a bushel basket full of records. But it wasn't simply *what* he did that made Johnny great—it was the *way* he did it that was truly spectacular. He was looked upon as

Johnny Unitas: Baltimore's Mister Quarterback.

football's finest clutch player, the greatest team leader, the man known as "Mister Quarterback."

Unitas was born in 1933 in a coal mining region of Pennsylvania. His father delivered coal for a living until he died when Johnny was five years old. From then on, Johnny's mother kept the family together, running the coal delivery business in winter and scrubbing office floors in warmer weather. Johnny helped out by running errands and doing odd jobs.

Johnny did pretty well in high school ball and hoped to get a scholarship to one of the bigger universities, such as Notre Dame or Indiana University. But he was too skinny to impress the major football powers and had to settle for the offer made by the University of Louisville.

As a college passer Johnny Unitas was pretty fair, although he was by no means a superstar. When he graduated in 1955, Unitas was way down on the draft lists. After more than 200 college players had already been picked, Pittsburgh finally decided to give the hometown boy a chance.

The tryout turned out to be nothing more than a quick look because the Steelers already had three quarterbacks. After he was cut, Unitas wrote letters to several other pro teams. The Cleveland Browns were the only team to show any interest, and even they wouldn't agree to consider him until they held next year's pre-season tryouts.

To keep in shape, Unitas hooked up with a sandlot team called the Bloomfield Rams, playing for six dollars a game. It was there that he came to the attention of the Baltimore Colts, who were shopping around for a spare passer. Don Kellett, a Colts executive, had seen

Unitas play and liked what he saw. He called Unitas and asked him to come to Baltimore. Later, Kellett was asked why he had picked up a player nobody else in the league wanted. Kellett grinned and said, "Where else could I have gotten a quarterback for the price of a telephone call?"

Unitas, with no major league experience, seemed destined for a lot of bench time. When the 1956 season began, the Colts appeared set with their regular quarterback, George Shaw. But in the fourth game of the season Shaw suffered a knee injury and had to be helped off the field. Coach Weeb Ewbank had no choice but to send in Unitas. He was as surprised as anyone when the rookie promptly ran off a streak of touchdown passes.

Shaw never did get his job back. That season, Unitas threw touchdown passes in three straight games. In 1957 he threw touchdown passes in every one of the twelve games he played. In 1958 he was in ten games and completed one or more touchdown passes in each of the games. In 1959 he played in twelve games and again tossed a touchdown pass in each of them. He continued connecting the same way for most of the following year. Then, on December 11, 1960, after throwing one or more touchdown passes in a record-breaking 47 consecutive games, he was finally stopped.

In 1958, while Unitas was in the middle of his touchdown streak, the Colts won the title in the NFL's Western Division. Baltimore went on to challenge the Eastern Division winners, the New York Giants, for the NFL championship. Millions of fans got an opportunity to see Unitas at his best—in one of the most exciting games in football history.

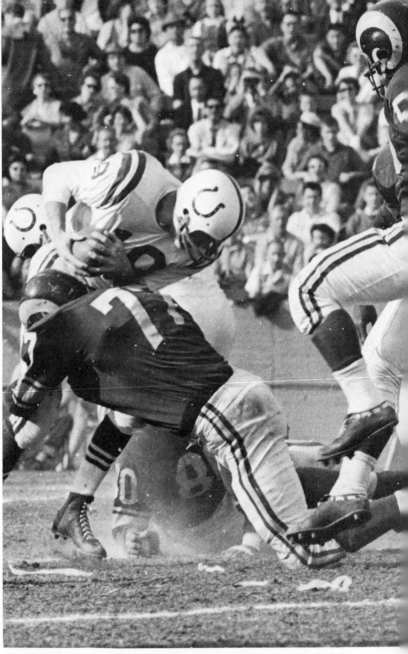

Unitas is thrown for a loss on December 11, 1960, the day his touchdown-throwing streak was ended at 47 games.

Baltimore was losing, 17–14, late in the final quarter. The Giants were faced with a fourth-down, foot-to-go situation, in their own territory. Deciding not to gamble, they punted. There was exactly 1 minute, 56 seconds left on the clock when Don Chandler's punt was downed on the Baltimore 14-yard line. The Colts had less than 2 minutes to score the tying field goal or the winning TD.

Johnny U and his teammates went to work. After missing his first couple of passes, Unitas proceeded to hit Lenny Moore for 11 yards, then zero in on receiver Ray Berry for passes worth 25, 16, and 21 yards. To save precious time, the last two plays were run off without a huddle, as Unitas tried desperately to lead the Colts downfield.

Now the ball was on New York's 13 and there was time for one more play. Baltimore's Steve Myhra booted the field goal that tied the game. For the first time in NFL history, a championship contest went into sudden-death overtime. The first team to score would win the game.

The Giants received the kickoff, but couldn't get a drive going. Don Chandler got off another long punt, this time into the Baltimore end zone. The Colts took over on the 20, and once again Johnny U went to work.

Now, because he had more time, Unitas could mix passes and running plays. Once he needed 8 yards for a key first down and saw Ray Berry out in the clear. But Berry was only 5 yards beyond the line of scrimmage. Unitas could have completed the pass and left it up to Berry to run for the extra yardage.

But Johnny hadn't worked this long and hard to leave anything to chance. Instead, he rolled out,

Johnny U (19) puts the ball in the air against the New York Giants.

holding the ball in his right hand and motioning with his left hand for Berry to move out deeper. Only then did he lay the ball into his receiver's hands for the big first down.

It took Baltimore 13 plays to score, with Unitas completing four out of five passes. On the final play, from 2 yards out, Alan Ameche slanted through a big hole in the line to give the Colts a 23–17 victory and the NFL championship.

There is no way to measure Johnny Unitas' contributions to the Baltimore offense. Whenever he was on the field the Colts were a threat, no matter what the score or how late in the game. But when Unitas got hurt and was out of action, Baltimore was a very ordinary team. The 1965 season illustrated that fact perfectly. With Johnny at the helm, the Colts won their first seven games and tied the eighth game. But in the ninth game, against Chicago, Unitas suffered a knee injury that finished him for the rest of the season. The Colts' fortunes took an immediate turn for the worse despite the efforts of Gary Cuozzo, then considered the best second-line quarterback in pro football.

This time the numbers really did tell the story. When the 1965 season ended, the Colts were 10–3–1. While Unitas was in action they'd had an 8–0–1 record. Without him they were 2–3–0.

Unitas was back in the line-up for the '66 season, and he continued to be the moving force behind the Colts for many more years. When the great Johnny took off his jersey and shoulder pads for the last time in 1973, he held seven passing records:

Most passes attempted, lifetime: 5,186
Most passes completed, lifetime: 2,830

Most yards gained, lifetime: 40,239
Most games, 300 or more yards passing, lifetime: 26
Most seasons leading league in touchdown passes: 4
Most touchdown passes, lifetime: 290
Most consecutive games, touchdown passes: 47

It's a funny thing about records: some can last a lifetime, while others change again and again over the years. For example, it's hard to imagine that Johnny's 1960 record of 47 straight games with one or more touchdown passes could be seriously threatened in the near future. On the other hand, his record for most passes completed in a single season, when he connected with 237 out of 410 in 1963, lasted just two years. John Brodie broke it in 1965 by completing 242 out of 391. But Brodie's record didn't last long either. In 1967 Sonny Jurgensen completed 288 passes. And by 1975 both Roman Gabriel and George Blanda had also passed Brodie's mark.

It is inevitable that some of Unitas' other records will be broken before long. By the mid-1970s, quarterback Fran Tarkenton of the Minnesota Vikings was already a strong threat in many departments (passes attempted and completed, yards gained, and touchdown passes). But no matter how many of Unitas' records he eventually upset, Fran Tarkenton would be the first to admit that there is something no one will ever take away from Johnny Unitas: the title of "Mr. Quarterback."

THE
SCORING
SPREE

On November 27, 1966, the New York Giants journeyed to Washington to play the Redskins. Both teams were also-rans, finishing out a disheartening season. The Redskins were 5–and–6, while the dreadful Giants were 1–8–1.

The dismal record of the Giants was largely due to the lack of a solid quarterback. The peerless Y. A. Tittle had retired after the '64 season, and the Giants had gone through a parade of passers since then. Earl Morrall was tried, but he didn't make it (although he later came back strong with the Baltimore Colts). Other Giant prospects included Glynn Griffing, Bob Timberlake, Gary Wood, and Tom Kennedy, but none of them could move the team. And the New York defense wasn't much more effective.

Washington, on the other hand, was weak on

defense but strong on the offense. The 'Skins had Sonny Jurgensen at quarterback, and when Sonny was right there was no one better in pro football. He could pick apart even the tightest defense, so the Giants weren't likely to give him much trouble.

The 50,000 fans who showed up to watch these two teams play could hardly have expected to see a record-breaking game—yet that's exactly what they saw. Things started out calmly enough. The Redskins took the kickoff, were unable to get going, and quickly punted.

New York coach Allie Sherman handed the starting assignment to quarterback Tom Kennedy, a rookie out of Los Angeles State. Kennedy got the Giants moving with a couple of line plays, but his first pass was intercepted by Washington defensive back Brig Owens. Then Jurgensen directed the Skins to a touchdown in half a dozen plays. The extra point attempt was blocked by New York tackle Jim Moran, so the Redskins led, 6–0.

Throughout the rest of the period the Redskins completely unnerved young Kennedy by either blitzing or pretending to blitz on every play. The Giants got the ball for three series of plays, but Kennedy failed to complete a single pass. Meanwhile, the Skins added another touchdown on a beautiful 63-yard burst by running back A. D. Whitfield. The quarter ended with Washington leading, 13–0, a very ordinary score.

For about half of the second quarter both teams pushed and pulled, huffed and puffed, all to no avail. Then the fun began. About midway through the period, Kennedy dropped back to pass again and his blocking dissolved. Washington linebacker Chris Han-

Early in the game, Giant quarterback Tom Kennedy runs into trouble—in the form of Washington's Chris Hanburger.

burger busted through and nailed the rookie so hard that he fumbled. Defensive back Brig Owens was on the spot again. He scooped up the football and raced 62 yards for the touchdown that put the Skins ahead 20–0.

Then it was New York's turn to get on the scoreboard. Kennedy hit receiver Homer Jones for 14 yards and Aaron Thomas for 35 more. Joel Morrison and Allen Jacobs did the rest of the job on the ground to make the score 20–7, Washington.

The Redskins couldn't score on their next drive, but they got the ball back quickly by intercepting another Kennedy pass. A. D. Whitfield carried the ball into the end zone, and after the kick, Washington led 27–7.

Then the touchdowns began coming in bunches. Another Kennedy pass, intended for receiver Bob Crespino, fell instead into the waiting arms of Washington defensive back Paul Krause. Joe Don Looney, a former Giant, took the ball in for the 'Skins. Score: 34–7.

Before the half ended the Giants managed to add another touchdown of their own. Quarterback Gary Wood took over for the rattled Kennedy and moved New York downfield with the help of a 45-yard pass interference call against Washington. Wood himself sneaked in for the TD from a yard out, and the half ended with the Giants on the short end of a 34–14 count.

Evidently coach Sherman said some harsh things to his men during the break, because the Giant offense started the second half with some fast and furious action. Phil Harris caught the kickoff on his 17 and bolted all the way to the New York 48 before being brought down. A pair of Gary Wood passes failed, but his next two clicked—first to Morrison for 11 yards, then right back to Morrison for the touchdown. After the placekick the score was 34–21.

The Giant defense was less successful, however. They just couldn't touch Washington's offense. As soon as the Redskins got the ball back they grabbed a fast TD, making the score 41–21.

Back came the Giants. Allen Jacobs and Joe Morrison carried, and Wood's pass to Homer Jones completed the drive. The scorekeeper counted all the points and posted the 41–28 score.

The give-and-take continued right after the following kickoff. A handoff to Whitfield actually lost a couple of yards, but then Jurgensen triggered the bomb to receiver Charley Taylor. Now the scoreboard read: Washington, 48–New York, 28. Apparently both teams needed a breather, because there was no more scoring in the third period.

The action started all over again shortly after the final period began, however. The Washington defense finally showed some muscle, forcing New York to punt. Then Rick Harris fielded the ball on the Washington 48 and went all the way for another touchdown. Now the Skins were leading, 55–28.

After an exchange of punts, New York had the ball again—but not for long. Wood tried a sideline pass. Once more Brig Owens was in the right spot at the right time. He stepped in front of the receiver, snatched his third interception of the day, and raced 62 yards for still another Redskin touchdown. Change the score again: Redskins, 62–Giants, 28.

At that point Giant coach Allie Sherman decided to

take Gary Wood out of the game and give Tom Kennedy another chance. After all, the game was lost anyway. Young Kennedy came through with four straight completions, missed one, then hit the next. Those passes and a couple of running plays, plus some Washington penalties, resulted in another New York touchdown. As the Washington fans cheered derisively, the point-after was missed. Now the scoreboard read 62–34.

Redskin Dick Shiner came in to give Jurgensen a well-deserved rest and promptly gave the ball away via an interception. With 1 minute, 35 seconds left, Danny Lewis scored for the Giants. But it was too little, and too late. By now the Giants were losing 62–41.

Even though the game was long out of reach, New York tried an onside kick, hoping for another shot at a score. It didn't work, though, and the Skins recovered on their own 47. Then the speedy Bobby Mitchell threaded his way through the entire Giant defense for still another touchdown. The harassed scorekeeper picked out the correct numbers and changed the board to read 69–41.

The scorekeeper wasn't the only one having trouble following all the action. Tom Kennedy was even more confused. With 7 seconds left on the clock, he threw the ball out of bounds, thinking that it was a third-down play and that he could stop the action. He did stop the clock—but it was a fourth-down play. Washington took over on the New York 22.

Then, as if the score wasn't high enough already, Redskin kicker Charlie Gogolak came in and booted a 29-yard field goal. That made the final score 72–41!

The total of 113 points was the highest ever scored

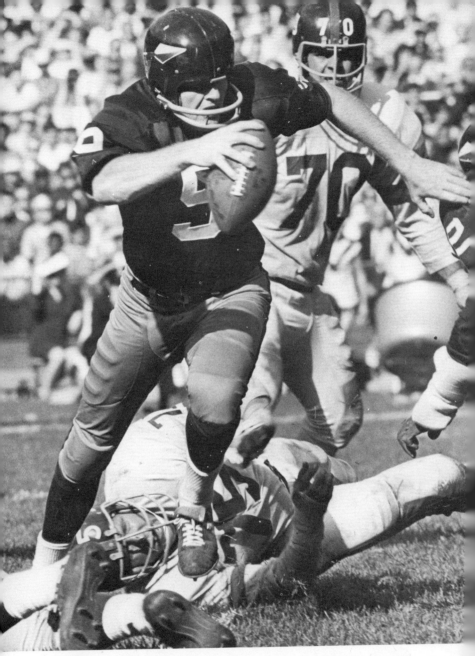

Redskin passer Sonny Jurgensen scrambles around—and over—the Giant defense.

by two teams in a single game. The Skins had racked up ten touchdowns, one field goal, and nine points-after-touchdown. The losers had scored an incredible six touchdowns and five points-after-touchdown. With any kind of defense at all, that should have been a winning effort for New York. But then, of course, the leaderless Giants would never have scored so many points if the Washington defense hadn't fallen down.

In all the excitement over the astronomical score, some other amazing statistics were almost overlooked. The Redskins, as host team, had to provide the game balls. During the super-scoring game 14 footballs were kicked into the stands. Another one was pitched to the crowd when Brig Owens did a jig of joy after his 62-yard interception. Altogether a total of 15 footballs disappeared that day. Official NFL footballs cost $22.50 each, so the lost balls cost Washington $337.50—which may well constitute another record!

ALL THE WAY WITH O.J.

Some sportswriters claim there is really no such thing as an individual record in football—only team records. And many players agree with that theory.

For instance, in 1974 quarterback Bert Jones of the Baltimore Colts broke the record for most consecutive passes completed in a single game, connecting for 17 in a row against the New York Jets. But, as Jones was the first to admit, he could never have done it all by himself. When he dropped back to pass, he needed—and got—fine protection from his line and blocking backs. His receivers had to be in exactly the right place at the right time, and when Bert threw, they had to catch the ball—and hold onto it. Without their support, there would have been no record.

Another star who was happy to share the honors with his teammates was Buffalo running back O.J. (Orenthal James) Simpson, also known as "Juice."

People living on the West Coast began hearing the name O.J. Simpson while he was still attending City College of San Francisco. In two years at that school he rolled up 2,445 yards rushing and scored 54 touchdowns. Then he enrolled at USC, where he began gaining national recognition. In 1968, his senior year, Juice established an NCAA record by rushing for 1,709 yards and won the Heisman Trophy, awarded to the college player of the year.

One of the reasons for Simpson's football stardom was his great speed. He was a sprinter on the USC track team, and in a 440-yard relay race, Juice and his mates set a world record of 38.6 seconds.

The Buffalo Bills made him their first draft choice in 1969. The Bills, who had once been AFL champs, had just concluded a miserable 1–12–1 season and were trying desperately to rebuild. They looked to O.J. Simpson to find the victory road. But as they soon learned, it takes more than one man—even one as great as Simpson—to make a winning team.

With O.J.'s help, Buffalo did improve in 1969—but just barely. The Bills finished the season with a 4–10–0 record—hardly cause for celebration. At that rate, it would be years before they had a winning season, much less a championship.

No one was more disappointed in O.J.'s rookie season than Simpson himself. An ordinary running back might have been satisfied with the 697 yards rushing, 393 yards catching passes, and 559 yards running back kickoffs gained by O.J. But O.J. Simpson was not just ordinary. He was supposed to be a superstar, the man who could break a game open with one lightning thrust.

Buffalo super-rookie O.J. Simpson got off to a slow start in 1969. Here he struggles for a one-yard gain against the Houston Oilers.

Of course, there were some good reasons for O.J.'s disappointing debut. First, there were the normal problems any rookie faces when he leaves college and becomes a pro—adjusting to a new coach, new teammates, and a new style of play. In O.J.'s case, the adjustment was doubly difficult because the Bills, under coach John Rauch, were used to playing a passing game. Buffalo's two strong-armed quarterbacks, Jack Kemp and Tom Flores, were more inclined to put the ball in the air than to hand it off.

Even though Rauch now had one of the greatest running backs to come along in years, he was reluctant to make any major changes in the Bills' game plans. Naturally, O.J. couldn't do much if he couldn't get his hands on the ball.

Despite these problems, Simpson got off to a good start in 1970. After seven games he was third in rushing in the AFC. He was averaging 15 carries a game and already had over 400 yards rushing. Then the Bills tangled with Cincinnati and O.J. was hit hard on a kickoff return. He suffered a knee injury and was lost for the rest of the season. Without him, the Bills finished 3–10–1.

Things didn't improve much in 1971. Still hoping to untangle the team, Buffalo fired coach Rauch and replaced him with Harvey Johnson, their director of player personnel. Everybody liked Johnson because he was such a nice guy. But head coaches in the pros must be more than just nice guys. Johnson had trouble disciplining the players, and team morale sank to an all-time low. Buffalo suffered through a 1–13 season, and O.J. gained 742 yards from scrimmage.

Then in 1972 two men came to Buffalo and turned the team around. One was head coach Lou Saban, who had coached the Bills to the AFL championship in 1965. The other was a 6-foot-4, 242-pound guard from Michigan named Reggie McKenzie.

Saban wanted to build the Bills with young players who would be eager to prove themselves and who wouldn't feel like losers. Rookie Reg McKenzie won the starting job at guard, rookie Bruce Jarvis took over at center, and Donnie Green, in his second season with Buffalo, was at tackle. Most important, Saban had big plans for O.J. He added several new ground plays to the Bills' book—all designed to get Simpson into the action.

Buffalo's renewed spirit was evident from the start of the '72 season. Although the young players made a lot of mistakes because of inexperience, they all hustled for the full 60 minutes of every game. And the player hustling hardest was O.J. Simpson. That year he led the entire NFL in rushing with 1,251 yards in 292 carries. It seemed that the more O.J. carried the ball, the more effective he was. The team finished with a 4–9–1 record.

The rest of the league realized that O.J. was indeed a threat to break open any ballgame. If they could stop him, much of the Buffalo attack would be gone. During the 1973 exhibition games, defensive units keyed in on him. It figured to be a rough season for Juice, but he was determined to make it even rougher for the opposition.

In the very first game of the regular season, O.J. Simpson served notice that he had come to play

The Bills' improved blocking gave O.J. some running room, and the great back made the most of it.

football. On a warm, sunny day the Bills took on the New England Patriots, and Juice showed everyone how a running back should operate.

He started slowly, twice going off left tackle for gains of 4 and 5 yards. He tried the right side twice for a total of 7 yards. And then everything clicked. With Reggie McKenzie blocking for him, Juice ran his favorite play—a sweep to the right. He took a handoff, streaked around the right side, and went 80 yards into the end zone. The play was so effective that the Bills used it eight times in a row during one stretch of the game. Each time, McKenzie cleared the way. And each time, O.J. picked up a few more yards.

Throughout that game O.J. flitted in and around the New England line, keeping the defense completely off balance. He went inside left guard for 3, off right tackle for 4, up the middle for 7, off right tackle again for 22, around left end for 11, around right end for 22. Altogether, in 29 carries, he racked up a total of 250 yards (a new record for a single game) to help the Bills to a 31–13 victory.

O.J. and the Bills had clearly surprised the Patriots with their aggressive running game. But their next opponents, the San Diego Chargers, were ready for them. The Chargers had watched films of the New England game and knew they would have to zero in on Simpson if they wanted to beat Buffalo. No matter where O.J. turned that day, the San Diego defense was waiting for him. He carried the ball 22 times, mostly for nibbles of 3 or 4 yards. Only three times was he able to roll up really good gains: once it was straight ahead for 14 yards, then around left end for 10, and then back up the middle for another 19. He did manage to gain 103 yards, but that didn't help the Bills, who were defeated, 34–7.

Game three, against the New York Jets, was almost a replay of the San Diego game for Juice, but this time Buffalo squeaked through with a 9–7 win. Again O.J. ripped off only three good gainers. The first time the Bills got the ball he went around right end for 15 yards; later, through center, he picked up 18 yards; and in the third quarter he went off tackle for 12 more. He also racked up a number of shorter gains, however, so by the end of the day O.J. had another 123 yards and 24 carries.

Next, against Philadelphia, O.J. showed how dangerous he could be in a tight squeeze. Buffalo had the ball on its own 42, second down with 27 yards to go. The Eagles figured a pass was coming, but Buffalo didn't have to pass with O.J. ready to go. Dashing straight through center, he picked up 29 yards and the first down. Right after that he went inside right guard for 28 yards more. Later in the period, Juice took the pitchout and rolled out to his right for an option-pass play. If he saw a receiver open, he was to throw, but if the chance came to run, he was to keep going. This time, however, all of Buffalo's receivers were covered and the whole right side of the Philadelphia defense was moving in on Simpson. But O.J. kept his cool and simply reversed his field, raced to his left, and picked up another 15 yards.

On those three plays Simpson added 72 yards to his total. And on 24 other carries he made 99 more yards for a game total of 171 yards—a major factor in the Bills' 27–26 victory.

In the following game, against Baltimore, Buffalo

picked up another win and Simpson picked up another 166 yards. Almost half of O.J.'s gain came on a single play when he ran the ball 78 big yards for his second touchdown of the day.

So far, in five games, O. J. Simpson had rushed for 813 yards. That would have been considered a nice *season* for most running backs. With a little luck he might go over the 1,000-yard mark before the season was half over.

But Buffalo's next opponents were the mighty Miami Dolphins, who were well on their way to an undefeated season. Juice never even got started against Miami. No matter where he turned, the whole Dolphin team seemed to be looking down his throat. He carried the ball only 14 times, picking up a mere 55 yards. It just wasn't his day. Nobody else on the team did any better, and the Bills were clobbered, 27–6.

O.J.'s next outing, against the Kansas City Chiefs, didn't figure to be any more profitable. The game was played on an AstroTurf field, and the artificial surface was slippery enough under normal conditions. But now it was raining, making the field even slicker than usual.

But this time O.J. refused to be stopped. In the first period Buffalo got possession on the Kansas City 15-yard line. Juice got the call four straight times. A fake reverse to the right gained 9 yards, a shot off tackle went for 2, off right tackle again gained 3 more, and then Juice went inside right guard for the TD.

Despite the difficult field conditions, O.J. Simpson ran at the Kansas City line time and again. They knew he was coming and braced to nail him. Four times he was stopped for no gain. Once he lost 4 yards, and another time he lost 2. But Juice kept pounding away, play after play, and his efforts paid off. By the time the game ended, he had gained 157 yards. He had carried the ball 39 times, a new NFL record for a single game.

The season was only half over, and already O.J. had gained 1,025 yards. Fans, sportswriters, and other players began to wonder if he could do as well in the second half of the season. That would put him over the 2,000-yard mark, a seemingly impossible achievement. Even the mighty Jimmy Brown had fallen short of that milestone; his best effort had been 1,863 yards.

O.J.'s dream seemed much farther out of reach after the eighth game, against New Orleans. The Saints had one of the league's weaker defenses, yet they managed to clamp down on Simpson and the Bills. Not only was Buffalo shut out, 13–0, but O.J. was held to 79 yards in 20 carries.

Game nine, against Cincinnati, was better for O.J., but not too good for the Bills. Buffalo lost, 16–13, but O.J. gained 99 yards. A good piece of the yardage came when Simpson and McKenzie teamed up for that old reliable end sweep to the right. This time it was good for 32 yards.

In the next game, the Bills suffered their third defeat in a row, getting shut out 17–0 by the Dolphins. But at least Juice was back into the 100-yard-game class again. He picked up exactly 120 yards, with 28 of them coming from the unstoppable Simpson-McKenzie supersweep.

The Bills found their way back into the win column with a victory over Baltimore, and O.J. added another 124 yards to his total. This time the sweep right went for 58 yards and a touchdown. Next, Atlanta played host to Buffalo and the Bills won, 17–6, as Juice rolled for 137 yards. He had long ago passed his mark of the previous season. In twelve games, Simpson had rushed for 1,584 yards.

Game 13 was O.J. Simpson's lucky game-number. He always did well against New England, and this time was no exception. Despite the raw, windy weather and the sloppy, wet AstroTurf, he ran for a whopping 219 yards. Of course Buffalo won, 37–13. And that big sweep play was working like magic. In the first period it was good for 24 yards. The play was called twice in the third period, good for 25 yards and then another 71. In the fourth quarter O.J. powered it for 28 more yards, and then, just for a change of pace, he went rambling on a sweep to the *left* for 25 yards.

That boosted O.J.'s season's total to 1,803 yards— just 60 short of Jimmy Brown's record and 197 yards from the 2,000 yard mark. With one more game still to be played, he was a cinch to break Brown's record. But he would need a super effort to hit 2,000.

It was another snowy, miserable day when the Bills played their final game against the Jets at Shea Stadium. But all the fans, all the players, and all the officials knew that O.J. Simpson was going to do a lot of running, snow or not.

Juice made headway immediately. The first time he carried, he went up the middle for 4 yards. Then he broke over right tackle for 30. The Jets knew all about that sweep right, and they were waiting for it. The play gained only 3 yards. But with Brown's record just out of reach, every yard counted. Juice kept pounding away, through center, off tackle, carrying the slippery football. Then on his eighth carry O.J. Simpson hit the left tackle slot and grabbed 6 yards to break Jimmy Brown's record.

By the end of the first quarter, O.J. had gained a total of 1,868 yards. He had 45 minutes of play to rack up another 132 yards for number 2,000, and he didn't figure to get it by gaining 4 or 5 yards per carry.

Simpson started the second period with a gain of 11 yards through left tackle. Then he tried his old favorite, the sweep right. But this time the play *lost* 2 yards. So it was back into the center again, banging into the tackle holes, nibbling away. Just before the halftime gun, Simpson ripped off a 13-yarder inside left tackle for a touchdown. That gave him a total of 42 yards for the period. But he still needed 90 yards in the second half.

Doggedly, his face and hands chilled by the 29-degree cold, O.J. Simpson kept chewing out the yards through the line. But he wasn't making enough headway with the short gainers. So late in the third period the sweep right was called again. This time it worked, and Simpson slithered and skidded his way along the sidelines for 25 big yards. The period ended with O.J. just 48 yards short of the magic mark.

But time was running out. Now it was the final quarter of the season for O.J. He hammered the line: 7 yards on a sweep left, off tackle for 2, back off tackle for a heartbreaking loss of 1. The Jets were closing off the middle. There was nothing to do but go back to the sweep right—good for 22 big yards. The 2,000-yard goal was in sight.

Next, Juice went into the left guard hole, only there

Against the Jets in 1973, O.J. goes for a new rushing record—with a little help from his friends McKenzie (67) and Delamielleure (68).

Surrounded by his teammates, Juice celebrates the end of his record-shattering season.

was no hole and no gain. Two runs around left end gave him 9 yards and then another 5.

And finally, with McKenzie and the entire team blocking like mad, Orenthal James Simpson pounded inside left guard for 7 yards. That did it for a grand total of 2,003 yards! And the game wasn't over yet. It seemed almost anticlimactic when the Bills finally won, 34–14. But that victory gave Buffalo a 10–4 record—their best since 1965.

In the 1973 season, O.J. Simpson had set eight records:

Most yards gained rushing, season: 2,003
Most yards gained rushing, game: 250 vs. New England
Most rushing attempts, season: 332
Most rushing attempts, game: 39 vs. Kansas City
Most games, 200 or more yards rushing, season: 3
Most consecutive games, 200 or more yards rushing, season: 2
Most games, 100 or more yards rushing, season: 11
Most consecutive games, 100 or more yards rushing: 7

In a press conference after the game, the room was jammed with people, all waiting to see one man—O.J. Simpson. Yet when he finally came in, Juice was not alone. With him was the entire Buffalo offensive unit. And he introduced them all, calling them by name, patting them on the back, thanking them for their help. Finally there was only one player he had not acknowledged, a big guard wearing number 67 on his jersey. Then O.J. said with a grin, "You all know my *main man*, Reggie—Reggie McKenzie!"

INDEX

Page numbers in italics refer to photographs.

147

148

Burkett, Jackie, 99

Cahill, Ron, 61
Cantor, Leo, 64
Card-Pitt, 63
   see also Chicago Cardinals and
      Pittsburgh Steelers
Carr, Roger, 72
Chandler, Don, 119
Chester, Ray, 31, 72
Chicago Bears, 24, 26, 46–54, 58,
   59, 62, 64, 67
Chicago Cardinals, 55, 56, 59–63,
   65, 121, 124
Chicago Cubs (baseball team), 95
Christman, Paul, 64
Cincinnati Gunners-Reds, 59
City College of San Francisco, 132
Cleveland Browns, 27, 32, 33, 58,
   67, 70, 77, 116
Cleveland Rams, 56, 59, 60, 63, 64
Conners, Dan, 106, 108
Conzelman, Jimmy, 61, 65
Cox, Fred, 42, 49
Crespino, Bob, 126
Csonka, Larry, 20, 22, 86, 87
Cuozzo, Gary, 38, 39, 44, 45, 121

Daddio, Bill, 56, 58
Dallas Cowboys, 55
Davidson, Ben, 105, 107, 108, 110,
   111, 113
Dawson, Len, 84, 85, 88, 89, 91,
   94, 108, 111, 140
Delamielleure, Joe, 68
Dempsey, Tom, 95–102, 98, 101
Denver Broncos, 33, 34, 70, 105,
   106, 108
Detroit Lions, 49, 50, 55–59, 57,
   61, 64, 69, 70, 99
Dixon, Hewritt, 33

Dodd, Al, 100
Domres, Marty, 70, 71
Dorais, Gus, 61
Dorou, Al, 79
Doughty, Glenn, 70
Durkee, Charlie, 97

Ebbets Field, 11
Edwards, Bill, 55
Eller, Carl, 37
Ewbank, Weeb, 71, 117

Fleming, Marv, 86, 87
Flores, Tom, 134
Foreman, Chuck, 20
Foxx, Jimmy, 123
Fuqua, Johnny, 15

Gabriel, Roman, 122
Gaubatz, Dennis, 41
Gifford, Frank, 77
Gilliam, John, 19
Gilliam, Sid, 96–97
Glacken, Scotty, 108
Goldberg, Marshall, 59
Gordon, Dick, 48
Grant, Bud, 38
Green Bay Packers, 27, 47, 49, 56,
   58, 59, 60, 61, 63, 105
Green, Donnie, 135
Green, Johnny, 79
Greene, Joe, 20
Greenwood, L.C., 19
Grier, Roosevelt, 48
Griese, Bob, 86, 87, 88, 89, 92, 111
Griffing, Glynn, 123
Grigas, Johnny, 62
Grim, Bob, 41
Grosscup, Lee, 79
Groza, Lou, 31
Gulyanics, George, 24